YORK NOTES

Learning Centre

Park Road, Uxbridge Middlesex UB8 1NQ
Renewals: 01895 853326 Enquiries: 01895 853344

UXBRIDGE
COLLEGE

The Return
of the Native

Thomas Hardy

Note by Kathryn Simpson

823.8

Kathryn Simpson is hereby identified as author of this work in accordance with
Section 77 of the Copyright, Designs and Patents Act 1988

YORK PRESS
322 Old Brompton Road, London SW5 9JH

PEARSON EDUCATION LIMITED
Edinburgh Gate, Harlow,
Essex CM20 2JE, United Kingdom
Associated companies, branches and representatives throughout the world

First published 2000
Seventh impression 2006

ISBN-10: 0-582-42454-2
ISBN-13: 978-0-582-42454-8

Designed by Vicki Pacey, Trojan Horse, London
Phototypeset by Gem Graphics, Trenance, Mawgan Porth, Cornwall
Colour reproduction and film output by Spectrum Colour
Produced by Pearson Education Asia Limited, Hong Kong

CONTENTS

PART ONE

INTRODUCTION

HOW TO STUDY A NOVEL

Studying a novel on your own requires self-discipline and a carefully thought-out work plan in order to be effective.

- You will need to read the novel more than once. Start by reading it quickly for pleasure, then read it slowly and thoroughly.
- On your second reading make detailed notes on the plot, characters and themes of the novel. Further readings will generate new ideas and help you to memorise the details of the story.
- Some of the characters will develop as the plot unfolds. How do your responses towards them change during the course of the novel?
- Think about how the novel is narrated. From whose point of view are events described?
- A novel may or may not present events chronologically: the time-scheme may be a key to its structure and organisation.
- What part do the settings play in the novel?
- Are words, images or incidents repeated so as to give the work a pattern? Do such patterns help you to understand the novel's themes?
- Identify what styles of language are used in the novel.
- What is the effect of the novel's ending? Is the action completed and closed, or left incomplete and open?
- Does the novel present a moral and just world?
- Cite exact sources for all quotations, whether from the text itself or from critical commentaries. Wherever possible find your own examples from the novel to back up your opinions.
- Always express your ideas in your own words.

This York Note offers an introduction to *The Return of the Native* and cannot substitute for close reading of the text and the study of secondary sources.

The Return of the Native is a story of extremes, of all-consuming passions and fierce ambitions, played out in the vast and overwhelming setting of Egdon Heath. It is a **tragedy** of ordinary lives: a family quarrel, romantic entanglements and the desire to escape are the elements which are brought together with a life-shattering intensity. Here, all life is a struggle for existence and the working of an apparently malign fate drives the story with a tragic inevitability. A foreboding atmosphere dominates most of the novel, and superstition and pagan rites contribute to the sense of the powerful forces which seem hostile to humanity, yet in control of human destiny.

Thomas Hardy's powers of description create a vivid impression of this living landscape and its inhabitants. Images of great beauty and great horror convey the extremes of human experience, and we are drawn into this world by the imaginative and intellectual engagement that the description demands. Hardy's use of language is poetic and stirs an emotional response in the reader, encouraging our sympathy for the characters and the pains and pleasures they experience. Hardy is at times also a master of suspense, involving us in his fictional world, and creating a sense of the mounting tensions the characters feel.

The Return of the Native addressed many of the intellectual and philosophical concerns of the Victorian period: concerns about God and belief, origins and destiny, and male-female relations. In this novel Christian belief is eclipsed by paganism, God does not exist and any belief in Providence is shattered. Hardy's characters live in an indifferent, if not hostile, universe. Victorian idealisation of Nature as synonymous with peace and innocence is likewise destroyed; Nature is ruthless and humanity is part of Nature. Hardy's female characters often break from the cultural ideals of femininity and his representations of intelligent and passionate women provoked censure from the critics. Eustacia is an intelligent hedonist, bored by her entrapment on the heath and desperate, ultimately gasping, for life. Likewise Hardy's depiction of illicit male-female relationships and his criticism of marriage made him a controversial figure, although he was always surprised when his writing was attacked for being subversive and immoral.

This points to an essential contradiction in Hardy; although he was radical in many ways, he also had a strong conservative tendency. This conservative tendency is clearly seen in his desire to record the culture of his native Dorsetshire; the depictions of life on Egdon Heath, the work, beliefs, festivities, superstitions, dialect and relationships between the heath folk in *The Return of the Native* intend to preserve 'a vanishing life'. *The Return of the Native* was written during the happiest period of his marriage and with the sense of relief that he felt on returning to his native Dorset. It marked a departure in Hardy's career as a novelist and is perhaps his most ambitious novel. It offers no easy solutions to the moral questions it raises, and the dramatic and passionate impression of life it creates is profound in its effect.

PART TWO

SUMMARIES

Thomas Hardy published four versions of *The Return of the Native* and it underwent several revisions. The serial version was published in the *Belgravia* magazine in twelve parts throughout 1878. Serialisation in the American *Harper's Magazine* ran between February 1878 and January 1879. The serial version was revised and published as a three-volume novel with the map of Wessex in Britain by Smith, Elder and Co. in November 1878, and in America by Henry Holt in December 1878. This version was used for the one-volume edition in 1879. The first collected edition of Thomas Hardy's works, the Uniform Edition, published by Osgood, McIlvaine in 1895 saw more revisions of the text and Thomas Hardy added a Preface. Hardy made his final revisions for the second collected edition, the Wessex Edition, published by Macmillan in 1912. To this edition he added a Postscript and the footnote concerning the modification of his original conception of the novel. This final version is the one usually used as a copy-text for modern editions, although the 1990 World's Classics edition of the novel is based on the three-volume first edition of 1878.

John Paterson and other textual critics have discovered much about the quite radical changes Hardy made to his manuscript and subsequent versions of the novel. For a discussion of the genesis of *The Return of the Native* see John Paterson's *The Making of 'The Return of the Native'*, University of California Press, 1960.

The text referred to in these Notes is the Penguin Classics edition, edited with an Introduction and notes by George Woodcock, 1985.

SYNOPSIS

On a November afternoon a reddleman travels with his cart along the lonely road which bisects the expanse of Egdon Heath. His conversation with an old man reveals that he is carrying a woman in his van; the local man guesses it is Thomasin Yeobright. After they part, the reddleman notices a figure on Rainbarrow, the highest point on the heath, and notes its disappearance when other figures arrive. These figures are the heath folk who have assembled on the barrow to celebrate 5 November, a festivity which owes more to its ancient pagan origins than to Guy Fawkes' Catholic conspiracy. Their **chorus** function is immediately apparent as their discussion introduces the main characters: Thomasin and Wildeve (the landlord of the Quiet Woman), who were to have married that day; Thomasin's aunt, Mrs Yeobright, who initially tried to prevent their engagement; Mrs Yeobright's son, Clym, who will return at Christmas; and Eustacia Vye, whose bonfire they can see and who is considered to be attractive but strange. We also get a good sense of the heath folk as individuals, especially Christian Cantle whose obsessive superstition makes him mistake the reddleman for a red ghost. The reddleman asks them whether there is a cart track to Mrs Yeobright's house. Shortly after he has gone Mrs Yeobright appears and leaves with Olly Dowden for the Quiet Woman, where Thomasin and Wildeve are due to arrive.

At the inn Mrs Yeobright meets the reddleman, Venn; Thomasin has not married because of a mistake over the licence. Mrs Yeobright demands an explanation from Wildeve, and in private Wildeve half-heartedly confirms his promise to marry Thomasin. The heath folk arrive from their bonfire in order to sing to the supposed newlyweds; Thomasin and Mrs Yeobright slip away unnoticed. When the heath folk have gone, Wildeve is tempted by Eustacia's signal (the fire which is still burning brightly) and he walks to Mistover Knap to meet with her. Eustacia has lit the fire to call her old lover to her, having gleaned from her grandfather (the man whom Venn met on the road) that Wildeve has not married Thomasin. On his way home Johnny Nunsuch, who had stoked Eustacia's bonfire, meets Venn and unwittingly reveals the secret meeting between Wildeve and Eustacia. Venn, a rejected suitor but still devoted admirer of Thomasin, decides to stop this relationship, and eavesdrops on Wildeve and Eustacia's next secret discussion on Rainbarrow.

The following morning he tries to persuade Eustacia to end her relationship with Wildeve and offers to help her to escape from Egdon, but she refuses. He tells Mrs Yeobright that he would like to marry Thomasin and she uses this information to put pressure on Wildeve.

Wildeve leaves her waiting for his decision and meanwhile renews his proposal to Eustacia that they leave for America. She in turn keeps him waiting; she realises that she does not want Wildeve now that the element of rivalry for his attentions has gone. The news of Clym's arrival from Paris, the place of her dreams, and the heath folk's matchmaking, which Eustacia overhears, shifts her attention to Clym.

Thomasin and her aunt prepare for Clym's arrival; Thomasin is now firm in her resolve to marry Wildeve. Eustacia passes Clym by chance as he returns home with this mother and cousin. Her fantastic and prophetic dream makes her determined to see him. She changes places with one of the mummers who are to perform at Mrs Yeobright's Christmas party. In disguise she speaks briefly to Clym and realises, without regret, that she has completely forgotten her meeting with Wildeve that night. Meeting Venn on the heath the following day, Eustacia makes clear that she wants to end her relationship with Wildeve; she sends Venn with a letter to him and returns his gifts. Infuriated by what he thinks is Eustacia's game-playing, Wildeve immediately goes to arrange his marriage to Thomasin, beating Venn who likewise intended to renew his offer of marriage. Wildeve and Thomasin marry two days later; Eustacia and Venn attend the wedding on purpose and Eustacia gives Thomasin away.

Clym is angry about not being informed of Thomasin's situation, which he has discovered whilst visiting a friend. His mother disapproves of Clym's plans to remain on Egdon to educate the heath folk, but Clym feels that the news of Eustacia being pricked as a witch by Susan Nunsuch strengthens his argument. Wondering whether Eustacia is the melancholy mummer and thinking she would be useful in his plans, he goes to help to retrieve the Vyes' well bucket. As Mrs Yeobright fears, Clym is attracted to Eustacia and over the next few months their relationship develops.

Mrs Yeobright's hostility to Clym's plans and her jealous disapproval of his relationship with Eustacia cause much friction; his proposal to Eustacia leads to a terrible breach and Clym leaves home. Thomasin's discussion with her aunt hints of her marital problems and Wildeve's refusal to give her any money. Meanwhile, news of Eustacia's imminent marriage revives Wildeve's desire for her. On the day of Clym and Eustacia's wedding, Mrs Yeobright decides to send both Clym's and

Thomasin's inheritance money to Mistover Knap in order to bring about
a reconciliation with Clym and to prevent Wildeve from appropriating
Thomasin's money. Christian Cantle is charged with the errand but, after
striking lucky in the raffle at the Quiet Woman, he gambles all one
hundred guineas away to Wildeve on the heath, whose initial motivation
is to take revenge on Mrs Yeobright for her lack of trust in him. Venn has
witnessed the game and wins all the guineas back but, not realising half
of them are for Clym, gives them all to Thomasin.

Eustacia and Clym live a secluded life in Alderworth; after the
first few weeks of romantic bliss, Clym resumes his studies and Eustacia's
hope of persuading him to return to Paris begins to fade. Mrs Yeobright
has received thanks for her gift from Thomasin, but not from
Clym. Eventually Christian confesses his gambling and Mrs Yeobright,
thinking that Wildeve may have passed on the money to Eustacia, goes
to meet her while she is visiting her grandfather. The meeting by the pool
results in a bitter quarrel; Eustacia returns home and demands to go to
Paris. Clym, in trying to achieve his goal of becoming a teacher more
quickly, temporarily damages his eyesight and takes up furze-cutting, to
Eustacia's anger and humiliation. To cheer herself up, she goes to a
'gypsying' and dances with Wildeve; returning home in the moonlight,
they see Clym and Venn approaching. Wildeve slips off home, but Venn
has seen him and beats him to the Quiet Woman. Venn's comments to
Thomasin indirectly inform Wildeve that he will try to stop his
relationship with Eustacia. Over the next few nights Venn trips Wildeve,
foils his moth signal to Eustacia, and shoots at him; Wildeve, therefore,
decides to visit Eustacia in the daytime.

Encouraged by Venn to seek reconciliation with her son,
Mrs Yeobright sets out across the heath in the blistering heat of
August 31. Resting outside Clym's house, she sees first Clym and then a
second man (Wildeve) enter. By the time Wildeve arrives, Clym is asleep
on the hearth, and the old lovers discuss Eustacia's unfortunate
situation. Thinking that the presence of a third person would ease
her visit, Mrs Yeobright knocks on the door. Eustacia is alarmed
when she looks through the window and sees Mrs Yeobright because she
thinks that Wildeve's presence will confirm her mother-in-law's
suspicion about their past relationship. They go into another room and,
when Mrs Yeobright knocks again, they hear Clym say 'mother' and

assume that he has answered the door. Wildeve leaves but when Eustacia goes back into the house, Clym is still asleep and Mrs Yeobright has gone.

Mrs Yeobright is physically and emotionally exhausted, and is accompanied part of the way home by Johnny Nunsuch. He leaves her when she sits down to rest. Meanwhile, Clym has awoken from a disturbing dream about his mother and determines to visit her that evening. On his way to Blooms-End, he finds his mother in a state of collapse. He carries her to a hut and goes to fetch help. The heath folk return with him and, discovering Mrs Yeobright's adder bite, apply a folk remedy. The doctor arrives, but cannot help her. Meanwhile, after her grandfather has informed Eustacia of Wildeve's inherited fortune of £11,000, she too goes walking on the heath. She meets Wildeve and they find themselves outside the hut. Unseen, they witness Mrs Yeobright's death. Johnny Nunsuch repeats the bitter words Mrs Yeobright had uttered when she thought that Clym had rejected her; Clym blames himself for her death.

Clym is very ill for several weeks as a result of his mother's death, and Eustacia has not revealed the truth of his mother's visit. One evening when Clym is much recovered, Christian comes to tell him that Thomasin has given birth to a little girl; he also reveals that Mrs Yeobright had intended to visit Clym on the day of her death. Two days later, Venn calls at Blooms-End, where Clym is busy sorting out his mother's things. He is shocked to hear of Mrs Yeobright's death and confirms that she was going to visit Clym to seek reconciliation. Clym discovers the whole truth when he questions Johnny again. He accuses Eustacia of cruelty and deception and she returns to her grandfather's house, where she contemplates suicide. On 5 November Charley, her grandfather's stable-boy and admirer of Eustacia, lights a bonfire to cheer her up and thus inadvertently signals to Wildeve. Wildeve offers to help her to escape to Paris. While Wildeve is out, Clym visits Thomasin who, with her own suspicions about Wildeve's infidelity, encourages Clym to write to Eustacia to seek reconciliation. Clym does so, but delays sending the letter until the following day.

The next evening Eustacia signals to Wildeve and he makes ready to leave at midnight. Thomasin's suspicions are aroused and she goes out to tell Clym of her fears about the situation. Fairway delivers Clym's letter too late, and Eustacia leaves without seeing it. Out in the stormy night, Eustacia realises that she has no money and feels thwarted in her bid to escape; at the same time, Susan Nunsuch melts an effigy of Eustacia. Captain Vye walks to Blooms-End to tell Clym that Eustacia has left; Clym sets out for the Quiet Woman, followed shortly by Thomasin who, getting lost on the heath, is helped by Venn. Venn has just heard a woman crying but could not find her, and Thomasin realises that it is Eustacia. A quarter of a mile from the inn, Wildeve is waiting for Eustacia and is surprised when Clym arrives. They hear the sound of a body falling into the stream close to the weir. Wildeve dives in when he sees Eustacia's body floating in the weir and is followed by the more cautious Clym; both are drawn into the strong currents at the centre. Venn and two other men manage to get all three out, but only Clym survives.

Thomasin and her baby, Eustacia Clementine, move back into the house at Blooms-End with Clym. About eighteen months later, Venn, now a dairy farmer again, returns to the heath. After a short courtship they marry and move to Venn's farm at Stickleford. Clym takes up his new vocation as an open-air itinerant preacher and preaches his first Sermon on the Mount on Rainbarrow.

BOOK FIRST: THE THREE WOMEN

CHAPTER 1   Egdon Heath is introduced

The novel opens in winter as the day approaches twilight. We are told that the isolated heath is 'a near relation of night' (p. 53) and seems to draw darkness to it; it is at night time that the heath's power is fully felt. The heath is described in terms of its ancient, unchanging and timeless qualities; its historical lineage surpasses any human record and human impact on it is minimal. It is a powerful, ominous and brooding place, always muting and darkening the light which does exist, and intensifying the storms and wind. It is also a psychological landscape, reminiscent of the 'wild regions of obscurity' (p. 55) experienced in nightmares. As the map which accompanied the first edition of the novel revealed, Egdon was based on a real geographical place, but it has **symbolic** meanings as well.

Unlike most other Victorian novels, the first chapter is not used to introduce the characters, although some critics have seen the heath itself as a kind of character, or at least an animate being. The heath is certainly established from the outset as a pervasive and active presence, and Hardy's repeated use of **personification** does accord it human qualities. The heath wears an 'antique brown dress' and has a 'lonely face' (pp. 56, 55). The factors of time and place, which are crucial to our understanding of the **plot** which will unfold, the characters, and the **themes** which will be explored are highlighted in this first chapter. The action of the novel is located in a specific historical context – the 1840s (as Hardy states in the Author's Preface) – and the chapter is framed by reference to the specific evening on which the story begins. Paradoxically, the vivid description in the rest of the chapter suggests that the heath has a crucial timelessness, however. The heath also seems indifferent, if not hostile, to humanity; yet, as we shall see, it also seems to feed the vitality of the heath folk. Such dualities and contradictions are found throughout the novel.

Hardy also draws attention to difference of this place from the **pastoral** settings of his own previous work, and from the more conventional depictions of rural idylls so popular with the Victorian reading public. The heath is said to appeal to a more modern perception and insight and, with reference to Victorian theories of evolution, it is suggested that as intellect evolves, so a different appreciation of what is beautiful will develop; this would include 'Haggard Egdon' (p. 54). Darwinian ideas clearly influenced Hardy's thought (see Historical Background) and recur throughout this novel. The parallel drawn between the heath and a prison, as new definitions of beauty are explored, anticipates Eustacia's feeling about this place (p. 54).

This description of the heath also suggests an empty stage set, and an atmosphere of expectation and anticipation is built up as the heath 'seemed to await something' (p. 54). **Allusion** to dramatic **tragedy** recurs throughout the novel emphasising the tragic events (see Narrative Techniques). In this detailed evocation of the setting for this novel, stressing that it is at night that the heath told its 'true tale', Hardy also prepares the reader for the dark and tragic tale he himself will tell: the heath, like this novel, has 'tragical possibilities' (p. 55). The white road which gleams so unnaturally amidst the gloom is the point of human entry to the heath, and our focus is shifted to it as the first characters appear on the scene.

furze-cutter furze is a shrub which is used for fuel; a furze-cutter gathers it

Vale of Tempe in classical times it was a proverbially beautiful Greek valley considered sacred to the god Apollo

Thule the northernmost land of which the ancient Greeks knew, it was cold, bleak and barren (possibly the Shetland islands)

Scheveningen a popular resort in the Netherlands; Thomas and Emma Hardy visited all three places in 1876 before they settled in Sturminster Newton

Leland appointed by Henry VIII in 1533 to search for historical records; he was judged to be insane and most of his findings were not published until the eighteenth century

Ishmaelitish in the Bible, Ishmael was the son of Abraham who was cast out into the desert (Genesis 16:12); it suggests that the heath is an outcast

vicinal way a local road

Via Iceniana, or Ikenild Street an ancient way stretching from Norfolk to Dorset which the Romans made into a major military road

CHAPTER 2 **As Captain Vye walks home, he meets Diggory Venn bringing Thomasin back to Egdon in his van. Venn sees Eustacia on the barrow. The characters are unnamed at this point**

As Captain Vye walks home, he meets the reddleman and they walk together in silence. Venn's concern for the contents of his van alerts Captain Vye to the fact that someone is inside it. A cry from the van prompts the Captain to question Venn, and Venn's abrupt responses reveal that he is carrying a woman. The Captain assumes it is 'that girl of Blooms-End' (p. 61) about whom there are rumours. Venn refuses to answer and they part company. As he surveys the landscape, Venn sees a solitary female figure on the top of Rainbarrow which leaves as other figures arrive there.

This chapter raises many questions as characters enter the scene along the road. The reader's curiosity is aroused by the reddleman, by the possible scandal attached to the woman in the reddleman's van, and by the relationship between them; the woman on the barrow invites questions, as does the activity of the others whose appearance prompts her to leave. The fact that the characters are unnamed and largely unexplored increases the reader's curiosity, and the use of **rhetorical questions** involves the reader in the mystery. The technique of introducing characters as distant objects in a vast landscape who gradually become identified as individuals is one Hardy uses in other novels, *Far From the Madding Crowd*, for instance. Here, it suggests the insignificance of human action on this landscape. The heath-as-a-stage idea is again hinted at as what Venn sees is referred to as a 'sky-backed pantomime of silhouettes' (p. 63), stressing the anonymity of the characters at this point.

As the highest point on the heath, Rainbarrow is a significant place for viewing the landscape. Its connection with the ancient human past is stressed here, and an imaginative stranger may initially fancy that the form on the top of the barrow was an ancient Celt. The fact that it is Eustacia who is so clearly identified as being part of this landscape, indeed completing the sense of harmony and unity of the view, is **ironic** given her feelings (shortly to be revealed) about the place and its inhabitants. The sense that Eustacia belongs to this place contradicts her ambitions for escape from the beginning. Both Eustacia and Venn are singled out in this chapter: Venn because his red colour stands out amongst the muted verdure of the heath, and Eustacia because she is at one with this paradoxical place. It is a place which has a 'healthy life' though resembles 'the torpor of death', and which 'exhibit[s] the inertness of the desert' whilst 'exercising powers akin to those of the meadow' (p. 62). The scientific terms used to describe Venn and his trade, 'the single atom of life' (p. 58) and 'extinct' (p. 59) and the reference to a species now extinct, the dodo, refers again to evolutionary ideas. The depiction of a traditional rural trade is also part of Hardy's preservation of the local history of Dorsetshire.

The narrative technique of shifting points of view, here Captain Vye's and Venn's, is used throughout the novel, and emphasises the idea of observation which is important later (see Narrative Techniques).

reddleman supplies farmers with the ochre dye used for marking sheep
Atlantean Atlas was a Greek demi-god who was strong enough to support the universe; Hardy is emphasising how small the barrow looks from the reddleman's perspective, even though in fact it was large
Celts the chief race in prehistoric Britain

CHAPTER 3   **The bonfire on Rainbarrow. The reddleman asks if there is a cart track to Blooms-End, Mrs Yeobright goes to the Quiet Woman and Eustacia's bonfire burns in the distance**

The figures on the barrow are revealed to be not 'intruders', as Venn and Eustacia seem to see them, but as the heath folk engaged in traditional Bonfire Night celebrations. They are introduced to us in the strange and shifting light of the bonfire; only gradually do we have a sense of their individuality as description moves from a general to a specific focus. Their conversation builds a sense of their individual characters and their gossip about Thomasin, Clym and Mrs Yeobright, Damon Wildeve, and Captain and Eustacia Vye and their relating of recent events provide much information for the reader. They discuss Thomasin's wedding to Wildeve and her aunt's attempts to prevent it; their hostility towards Mrs Yeobright is apparent. They give their opinions about Thomasin, Wildeve, Clym (who is to return at Christmas), as well as about Captain and Eustacia Vye. Their lack of Christian faith is apparent, as is their strong sense of superstition; Christian Cantle is especially, and somewhat comically, fearful and accepts his destiny, caused by his birth on a moonless night, as 'The man no woman will marry' (p. 75). Venn approaches them to ask whether there is a track suitable for a cart to Mrs Yeobright's house. When he has gone, Mrs Yeobright then appears and leaves with Olly Dowden to go to the Quiet Woman (where Wildeve is landlord). Following sprightly Grandfer Cantle's lead, the heath folk go to sing to the newly married couple.

The heath folk have a strong relationship with the heath and their activities form a continuum with the past. Their ritual fire and dancing associates their activities with more ancient pagan rites, and their participation seems to seal their bond with the heath (as they burn the faggots cut from it), and with surrounding communities, with the fires acting as signals. There is a strong sense of community spirit expressed here and private celebrations of what could be communal (Thomasin and Wildeve's marriage and Eustacia's bonfire) offend against this social spirit. Unlike the main characters, they speak using Dorsetshire dialect and again Hardy's preservation of his local heritage in terms of language and customs is apparent. Although the heath folk are frequently depicted in a comic way, they have a very important function and act like a Greek **chorus**, commenting on the actions, tensions and antagonisms of the main characters. We gain crucial information here about the relationships between the main characters and discussion of Clym's return builds a sense of expectation.

Maenades the frenzied women devotees of Dionysus
Limbo ... vision Dante (1265–1321) was born in Florence and was the major Italian poet; in his *Divine Comedy* Limbo is the first circle of the Inferno, an intermediate region between heaven and hell reserved for the souls of the pious who died before the time of Christ
Thor the Old Norse god of thunder
Woden the chief deity of Anglo-Saxon pagans; both Celtic and Anglo-Saxon pagans lit fires to mark the beginning of winter
Promethean Prometheus was a Titan in Greek mythology who made humans out of clay and stole fire from the gods on Olympus; he was punished by Zeus, who chained him to a rock where a vulture picked at his liver everyday
Dureresque Albrecht Dürer (1471–1528) was a German painter
'The king ... may be' from a seventeenth-century West of England ballad, 'Earl Marshall'; later Grandfer refers to the 'Jovial Crew', another name for this ballad
'I'll go shrive the queen' 'I'll go to hear the queen's confession'
stave song
weasand throat
three sixes eighteen

jowned damned

vell nor mark trace

forbad the banns the banns are a public declaration of an intended marriage issued in a church on three consecutive Sundays; anyone who objected could make their opinions known; Mrs Yeobright tried to stop the marriage of Thomasin and Wildeve

set-to relationship

in the mangling developing

leggings ... brass Goliath, the giant in the Bible whom David kills, wore brass armour on his legs (Samuel 17:6)

nunny-watch fuss

to-year this year

tide-times festival times

Bang-up Locals 'bang-up' is an obsolete term meaning 'first rate' and the Locals were the Dorsetshire Yeomanry, first formed in 1794; they were called to be ready to defend at several times during the Napoleonic wars, notably in 1804

zid saw

dog-days between July 13 and August 11 when the dog star rises and sets with the sun; the hottest time of the year

strawmote a single blade of straw

stunpoll fool

to tear her smock to leave home

gallicrow scarecrow

maphrotight hermaphrodite

tattie-digging the time of the potato harvest

Lammas-tide the early English Church's harvest celebration which takes place on August 1; descended from earlier pagan festivals

rames skeleton

Wethers castrated rams

ballet ballad

dry as a kex needing a drink; a kex is the dry, hollow stem of a plant

nammet-time lunchtime

cleft-wood wood chopped for fuel

knap summit of a small hill

zany fool or simpleton

outstep remote, lonely

mandy impertinent, cheeky

vlankers sparks

poussetted danced around with joined hands

mommet strange figure or effigy

Nebo in the Bible, the summit of the mountain on which Moses stood and heard the words of God, and from which he saw the Promised Land (Deuteronomy 3)

huffle to blow in gusts

pixy-led to be led astray by pixies or fairies; to be lost or confused

CHAPTER 4   **Mrs Yeobright meets the reddleman and Thomasin is revealed to be the woman in his van**

On the way down from the barrow Mrs Yeobright tells Olly that her consent for Thomasin to marry Wildeve was given unwillingly. As Mrs Yeobright is about to enter the inn, the reddleman approaches her and she recognises him as Diggory Venn (thus naming him for the first time), who is the son of a local dairyman. Venn informs her that he has Thomasin (also named for the first time) in his van and that she has fainted and is upset. When Venn has left, Mrs Yeobright sternly demands an explanation.

Doubts about Wildeve's suitability as a husband for Thomasin continue to be expressed by Olly, whose comments about Wildeve's failure in his former occupation suggest his arrogance. Doubts about his character are also raised by the comments about the plot of land called 'Wildeve's Patch' which was laboriously reclaimed from the heath and cultivated at the expense of two men's lives. Likened to Amerigo Vespucci, Wildeve reaps the benefits of other men's labour and sacrifice and is suggestively an exploitative character. By contrast, Venn is kind and considerate in his treatment of Thomasin and sensitive to what is appropriate behaviour (p. 89). There is a hint of some former relationship between Venn and Thomasin, which resulted in his turning to the lonely and transient trade of reddleman (Venn's bitter comment concerning his unsuitability to be Thomasin's husband in the second chapter similarly suggest this, p. 60).

From the comments of the heath folk we have a sense that Thomasin is well-liked, and her innocent beauty and gentle vitality are emphasised. She is in many ways a typical **pastoral** heroine, identified as she is with nature, her 'honest country face' and 'nest' of hair, and with the harmony of madrigal music, often associated with pastoral texts (p. 89). She represents the 'fair' and angelic heroine who is frequently set in opposition to a dark, demonic female character in Victorian fiction; Eustacia is clearly the *femme fatale* to Thomasin's Victorian feminine ideal and contrasts between them are repeatedly drawn throughout the novel (see Characterisation).

Tartarean in Greek and Roman mythology Tartarus was the lowest region of hell; it emphasises the heath folk's descent in the darkness of the heath
Amerigo Vespucci the Italian explorer after whom America was named, although others discovered it before him

CHAPTER 5   **Thomasin and Mrs Yeobright enter the inn where Wildeve explains the mistake about the wedding licence. The heath folk arrive to sing and wish the couple joy**

Thomasin tells her aunt that she is not married and, in a hostile mood, Mrs Yeobright demands an explanation from Wildeve. Wildeve explains that he and Thomasin could not marry because their licence only allowed them to be married in Budmouth, not in Anglebury where they had gone. Alone with Wildeve, Thomasin apologises for angrily leaving him that morning, but although he says he will still marry her, the antagonism between him and Mrs Yeobright threatens to jeopardise their union. There is also a distinct undercurrent of uncertainty in his promise. The heath folk arrive singing to wish the newlyweds joy; Mrs Yeobright and Thomasin remain in the parlour while Wildeve resentfully keeps up the pretence of being married and offers the heath folk mead. Much eulogising about Thomasin's father's goodness and his great musical talents ensues, with a sense of sadness at his sudden death. After they leave, Wildeve returns to the parlour, but Thomasin and her aunt have gone. He remembers his promise of giving a bottle of wine to Olly Dowden's sick husband and he goes out to leave it in their house. Seeing Eustacia's 'signal light' (her bonfire) still burning he walks towards her house at Mistover Knap.

Mrs Yeobright's quick shifts of mood and manner are made explicit, and her hostility to and deep suspicion of Wildeve are made clear. The antagonism she arouses in Wildeve does threaten to damage his relationship with Thomasin; this anticipates the damage her manner will cause later in her interaction with Eustacia. Her distrust of Wildeve is deserved when his clandestine relationship is revealed. We gain a strong impression of Wildeve's character in this chapter: he is physically attractive to women, but seems to cruelly toy with Thomasin's feelings and fears. He does not entirely relieve her anxieties about their marriage as he gives his promise to marry her the following Monday 'carelessly' (p. 96). The situation with the arrival of the heath folk is clearly an uneasy one, but the fact that they don't seem to perceive his cold response to them as unusual suggests that he always assumes the condescending and supercilious attitude to them that we see here. His manner contrasts starkly with their cheer, exuberance and genuine feeling; although their taste and judgement is seemingly undermined by the references to recognisably 'great' performances of Farinelli and Sheridan (p. 100).

Thomasin's attitude to her relationship with Wildeve is a practical one; unlike the excessively romantic ideas of Eustacia (as we see in the following chapter) Thomasin recognises that reality is not 'pretty and sweet' (p. 95). Her anxieties about not being married are also grounded in the reality that it would mean a ruined reputation; her fears that the singing of the heath folk may mean a 'skimmity-riding' suggest her fear of the public knowledge of her situation. Her anxiety could also be about marrying Wildeve at all, since there are hints here, which are more definite later, that she does not love him.

The description of Rainbarrow seeming to loom over the inn adds a sense of foreboding to Wildeve's involvement with the figure we saw there earlier (p. 92). This past relationship casts a shadow over his relationship with Thomasin, and ultimately results in **tragedy**.

by my crown by God

skimmity-riding a procession in order to expose an unfaithful spouse to ridicule; one of the participants impersonates a wronged or wronging spouse

heling pouring

the Hundred-and-thirty-third the 133rd Psalm was put into verse by Nahum Tate and set to music by Nicholas Brady, 'Lydia' is a common hymn tune

Farinelli Carlo Broschi (1705–82), a famous eighteenth-century singer who sang to the Spanish king, Philip V, for ten years to cure the king's depression

Sheridan's renowned Begum speech Richard Brinsley Sheridan, a dramatist and statesman, delivered a five hour speech in 1787 charging Warren Hastings with extorting funds from the princesses (begums) of Oudh

gown-piece fabric used for making a dress

slittering skipping along

mossel morsel, hint

fess lively, strong

scattered confused, frightened

We have been told ... deliberates a line from Joseph Addison's *Cato*: 'The woman that deliberates is lost' (IV, i)

CHAPTER 6   **Eustacia returns to the barrow and then goes home. Wildeve is drawn by her signal fire and they meet outside Eustacia's house and discuss their feelings**

Attention now shifts to the figure on the barrow who has returned after the heath folk have gone to the inn. Eustacia's appearance and personality are gradually revealed to us, and eventually her reasons for standing on the barrow with a telescope and an hour-glass become apparent. She waits alone, tense with expectation, and then with sure-footed familiarity returns to Mistover Knap where Johnny Nunsuch is reluctantly feeding her bonfire. He is sent away with a sixpence for reward when Wildeve signals his arrival. Eustacia and Wildeve part after a short but emotionally charged discussion, and it is revealed that they have been lovers. Hearing of Thomasin's return from her grandfather, Eustacia has lit her signal fire because she thought Wildeve had been faithful to her in not marrying Thomasin. At first she is triumphant about the power she has over him, but knows that 'he trifled with her', and when he refuses to commit himself to her, she sends him away and goes to bed crying (p. 117).

Eustacia is ladylike and adopts a commanding attitude towards her grandfather and Johnny – 'she was absolute queen here' (p. 110) –

yet she is also young and petulant. Her exchange with Wildeve reveals her to be proud, arrogant and changeable. She refers to herself as 'the witch of Endor' (p. 116), recalling a similar comment made by Timothy Fairway which suggests a certain hostility towards this mysterious figure (p. 101). Using reference to the classical and historical figures of Sappho and Mrs Siddons, Eustacia's romantic and tragic possibilities are suggested, as is her capacity for genuine passion and dramatic pretence. The heath at night is potentially a fearful place, a sense of which is evoked by the gruesome **image** of the embers of the heath folk's bonfire when Eustacia returns to the barrow, 'the red coals of the perishing fire greeted her like living eyes in the corpse of the day' (p. 104). The vivid description of its dead foliage in winter adds to the ominous atmosphere: the 'mummied heath-bells ... dried to dead skins by October suns', and the moaning music of the wind as it blows over them which resembles 'the ruins of human song' (p. 105). Eustacia is not afraid, however, and again seems to be in harmony with the heath: her sigh blends in with its musical 'discourse' and she is embraced by the night (pp. 106, 107). Her ability to negotiate the heath at night is a result of her intimate knowledge of this landscape and when a bramble catches her skirt she is said to 'yield herself up to the pull', suggesting also her despondent mood (p. 108).

Despite this harmony, however, Eustacia desperately longs to escape from the heath which she considers to be a prison. The objects she holds and the use she puts them to **symbolise** this. One hope of escape is to leave the heath with Wildeve (a plan which has tragic consequences later), and she uses the telescope to see if Wildeve is approaching and the hour-glass to measure the time she has waited for him. The hour-glass and the telescope also symbolise her antagonism to the heath at another level: she resents the power that it seemingly has to control time and space; its timelessness and intense hold over its inhabitants frustrate Eustacia's desires and she longs to take back some measure of control in order to exert her will. We also discover later that both of these objects are associated with life beyond the heath; the hour-glass was her mother's and the telescope her grandfather's, presumably used when he was a sailor (p. 124). Eustacia's contradictory relationship to the heath is at the heart of her **tragedy** and is repeatedly alluded to; her failure to escape its power is thus predicted from the outset. Her feelings for Wildeve also reveal the 'strange warring' within her and the use of light and dark imagery (used frequently in this novel) here emphasises the conflict in Eustacia between reason/will and her instincts and passionate nature: with the 'electric light' of reason she realises her mistake in loving Wildeve, but 'she loved on' (p. 117). The repetition of this phrase emphasises that what is uppermost in Eustacia's character is her instinctual passion and her association with dark strange forces.

Caesar Julius Caesar (102–44BC) invaded Britain in 55BC but withdrew his troops in the winter

Cimmerian land a mythical land which Homer claims is one of perpetual darkness

Sappho the Greek lyric poet of the seventh century BC who lived on the island of Lesbos; she is said to have committed suicide by drowning herself because a male lover rejected her

Mrs Siddons Sarah Kemble Siddons (1755–1831) was a great tragic actress

redan a fortification in which two defences meet at an angle pointing away from the centre

the hand ... Belshazzar in the Bible, Belshazzar was the last Babylonian king who saw the hand of God write words predicting his doom on the wall (Daniel 5)

parian fine white marble from the Greek island of Paros

Albertus Magnus Albert von Böllstadt (c.1193–1280) was a theologian and natural scientist who is said to have made a brass statue move and chatter

crooked sixpence supposed to ward off evil

Hypocondriasis a morbid state

Witch of Endor in the Bible, King Saul instructed the Witch of Endor to call up the spirit of the dead Samuel, who foretold Saul's death on the following day (Samuel 28:3–20)

CHAPTER 7   Detailed description of Eustacia's appearance, character and origins

The chapter begins with a richly poetic description of Eustacia's appearance. We are told about her background; her father was a Greek bandmaster in a British regiment, but when both of her parents died she was forced to move from the fashionable seaside resort of Budmouth to live with her grandfather on Egdon Heath. Her background, education and experience in part explain the extremes of her character, 'There was no middle distance in her perspective' (p. 120), and the oddness that many of the other characters perceive. She feels like a prisoner on Egdon and her proud and dignified attitude is a result of her intense loneliness. Loneliness in turn fuels her passionate desire for a powerful, all-consuming love; although she knows that she will be disappointed, the satisfaction of her longing is a matter of survival for her and she longs for it 'as one in a desert would be grateful for brackish water' (p. 122). She is rebellious, but the heath turns her vitality to gloom. She idealises Wildeve only because she has no other object on which to focus her dreams and desires; he could easily be supplanted by 'the advent of a greater man' (p. 123).

> The language and images used to describe Eustacia are inflated in order to convey her strange and contradictory qualities, and Hardy draws on a wide range of reference to convey the complexity of her character. She is 'the raw material of divinity' and 'a model goddess', if not 'a model woman' (p. 118). Associated with the enigmatic Sphinx, Greek goddesses and Pagan mysteries, a sense of her beauty, sensuality, power, exoticism and intensity is evoked, as is her arrogance and indifference, and even cruelty. The opening paragraph makes clear that if Eustacia did have power, she would not make the world a fairer place – a contrast with Clym's socialistic intentions later. Although 'Egdon was her Hades', it does satisfy some of her sensual longings and the rich language which associates her with nature and with night (especially her hair, p. 118) again confirms her connection with the heath. In fact, since she has lived there she has absorbed 'much of what was dark in its tone', although she is in harmony with it against her will (p. 119).

Although some critics have found Hardy's style clumsy, in his description of Eustacia the rhythm and balance of his writing is as important as his words and images in conveying a sense of her complexity. In describing her mouth, for instance, Hardy uses repeated phrases to build a sense of how her private vulnerability becomes publicly manifested as passion and arrogance, which is then perceived as scorn: 'The mouth seemed formed less to speak than to quiver, less to quiver than to kiss. Some might have added, less to kiss than to curl' (p. 119).

Olympus home of the gods in Greek mythology
the distaff, the spindle, and the shears the three Fates, or Greek goddesses, who decide human destiny; Clotho was the spinner and was responsible for birth, Lachesis used a spindle to unwind the thread of life, and Atropos used shears to cut the thread
Sphinx a statue with the head of a woman and the body of a lion; renowned for being mysterious and enigmatic
Ulex Europoeus the Latin name for furze or gorse
cima-recta, or ogee an architectural term for an s-shaped moulding
Sleswig a city in Germany which was the original home of some of Britain's Anglo-Saxon invaders
lotus-eaters in Homer's *Odyssey* some sailors ate the lotus fruit which induced a drugged state of languor
the march in 'Athalie' Handel's famous march composed in 1733 for Racine's last tragic drama
Artemis, Athena, or Hera Greek goddesses: Artemis was a virgin goddess and a huntress, Athena was the goddess of war and wisdom – both resisted being conquered by love; Hera was the jealous wife of Zeus, and the goddess of marriage, sex and childbirth
Hades in Greek mythology it was the place of the dead or hell
Richter Johann Paul Richter (1763–1825) was a German writer
Corfiote a native of Corfu
Alcinous king of Phaeacia (thought to be Corfu) was the father of Nausicaa who helped Homer's hero, Odysseus
Fitzalan and De Vere well-known aristocratic families of high repute
'a populous solitude' a quotation from one of Hardy's favourite poems, Byron's 'Childe Harolde' (i

William the Conqueror defeated King Harold in 1066 and became King of England; he was at war throughout his reign

Strafford Thomas Wentworth, Earl of Strafford (1593–1641) executed in 1641

Napoleon Bonaparte the French Republican leader who was defeated at Waterloo in 1815

Saul, or Sisera biblical leaders who lived violent lives and died tragic deaths (2 Samuel 1, Judges 4)

Jacob or David biblical leaders who were respected

Pontius Pilate in the Bible, he gave Jesus over to the Jews to be crucified; Eustacia's choice of heroes demonstrates her preference for the romantic, nonconformist and unpopular

Delphian the oracle of Apollo gave answers in riddles

Héloïses Héloïse (1101–64) was celebrated for her pure and constant love for the theologian, Peter Abelárd (1079–1142); their remains now lie together

Cleopatras Cleopatra is said to have deceived both of her lovers, Julius Caesar and Mark Anthony

CHAPTER 8   Johnny Nunsuch tells Venn what Eustacia and Wildeve have said at their secret meeting

As Johnny walks home alone, clutching his sixpence for courage, he becomes alarmed by the unusual light, dust and noise from what he later realises is Venn's van. Returning to Eustacia's house, he overhears the discussion between Eustacia and Wildeve and, afraid of angering Eustacia by interrupting them, he once again sets off for home. Spying on Venn, he falls into the ditch where Venn has set up camp. Whilst Venn bandages Johnny's wound and allays his superstitious fears about reddlemen, Johnny unwittingly reveals Eustacia's secret signal and her meeting with Wildeve, and relates the snippet of conversation he has overheard. Venn, of course, realises the implications of this as Johnny, a child, cannot. Venn goes part of the way home with Johnny.

From his child's point of view Johnny does not realise the implications of what he has done and seen. Venn, already seeking some explanation for the figure on the barrow, Eustacia's fire and Thomasin's failed attempt to marry Wildeve, instantly recognises the significance of what Johnny reports. Johnny will later play a similar role when he accompanies the dying Mrs Yeobright part of the way home and later relates what she has said to him. In both instances, he reveals information about Eustacia which is detrimental to her. Other coincidences continue to play a key role in the development of this **plot** and suggest the element of chance which is central to human life (see Recurring Themes).

Scyllaeo-Charybdean position in Greek mythology the Strait of Messina, off the coast of Sicily, had two dangers for sailors – Scylla (a dangerous rock) and Charybdis (a whirlpool); both were represented as female monsters. The phrase describes a situation in which any course of action is dangerous or unpleasant

CHAPTER 9   **Venn spies on Eustacia and Wildeve and resolves to speak to Eustacia**

After a quasi-historical description of the dying trade of selling reddle, there are suggestions of what motivated Venn to take up this trade. The virtually complete isolation which it brings, and the hint of a degree of self-inflicted punishment seem to have played a part in Venn's decision. Thomasin's refusal to marry him (revealed as he rereads her letter, written two years previously) is another factor; as a reddleman he can be near her yet unnoticed. With the intention of altruistically helping Thomasin to marry Wildeve, Venn waits for the lovers (Eustacia and Wildeve) on the barrow every night of the following week; it is not until Saturday that they appear. Venn eavesdrops on their conversation; he discovers that Wildeve is still not married to Thomasin and that he is torn between her and Eustacia. Wildeve and Eustacia discuss their hatred of the heath and Wildeve proposes that they escape to America. They part and Venn returns to his van, planning to see Eustacia.

The lovers' conversation reveals the power struggles which seem to be at the heart of their relationship. At first Wildeve seems to be in control and plays on Eustacia's insecurities, but the balance swings as Eustacia asserts the power she has over him. What unites them is their loathing of the heath. The **imagery** adds a sense of foreboding to this meeting; the sound of the wind is associated repeatedly with death: 'It was as if the night sang dirges with

clenched teeth' (p. 137), and the wind blows 'mournfully' (p. 139).
It also anticipates their failure to escape, since they seemingly are
part of the body of the heath; as they leave the barrow it is as if they
are 'two horns which the sluggish heath had put forth from its
crown, like a mollusc, and had now again drawn in' (p. 140). The
imagery builds up a sense of anticipation of death, which Eustacia's
words prophetically clarify: ''Tis my cross, my shame, and will be
my death!' (p. 139).

The description of the letter that Venn has kept also evokes the
immense sadness Venn feels about Thomasin's refusal. It is now
tinged with red (as it would be expected), just as Venn's life is
permeated with sadness: 'the black strokes of writing thereon
looked like twigs of a winter hedge against a vermilion sunset'
(p. 133). Both 'winter' and 'sunset' signal an end (of the year or of
the day), and the colour red, associated with passion and romance
(especially in the context of a sunset) signals the loss of these when
he received this letter. Venn has assumed a red with very different
associations in choosing the reddle trade (as the discussion at the
beginning of the chapter suggests). Mrs Yeobright's interference
and sense of superiority played a part in this thwarted relationship;
a similar intervention later in the relationship of Clym and Eustacia
has far more tragic consequences.

In his discussion of the trade of the reddleman Hardy is making a
very explicit record of this dying trade and the local customs and
superstitions associated with it, just as in the following chapter he
is providing an ornithological record.

Mephistophelian Mephistopheles is the name for a devil
Arab in this context means nomadic
Cain in the Bible Cain killed his brother Abel; God marked him so that no
one would kill him and condemned him to wander alone for the rest of his
life (Genesis 4:1–16)
ewe-lamb as in Nathan's parable to David about a rich man who steals a
poor man's single beloved ewe (2 Samuel 12); meaning a valuable
possession
Tantalus in Greek mythology he was punished with perpetual thirst and
hunger for revealing the secrets of the gods. He was forced to stand up to

his chin in water under a tree laden with fruit; the water receded when he tried to drink, and the fruit was just out of reach

CHAPTER 10   **Venn tries to persuade Eustacia to give Wildeve up, but she refuses**

Early the following morning Venn goes to Eustacia's house. When she eventually emerges, Venn flatters her in an attempt to persuade her to intercede in the 'trouble' between Thomasin and Wildeve on Thomasin's behalf. This fails and Venn is forced 'to play the card of truth' (p. 145). Eustacia is shocked when he reveals that he has overheard her discussion with Wildeve, but refuses his plea to give up Wildeve and be beaten by 'an inferior woman' (p. 146). The prospect of escape to Budmouth which Venn offers is momentarily tempting, but Eustacia refuses to work or give up the independence she has on the heath. Venn leaves hopelessly disappointed and, with renewed determination and regardless of possible scandal, Eustacia 'impetuously' asserts her intention to 'never give him [Wildeve] up – never!' (p. 149).

Venn's kindness, generosity and consideration form a constant contrast to the selfish arrogance of other characters throughout. Although Venn is said to lack the 'gallantry' which is part of what attracts women to Wildeve, he is 'astute' in a way that the charming and arrogant Wildeve is not (p. 142). Here his altruistic actions in trying to persuade Eustacia to give up Wildeve contrast strongly with her selfish reasons for holding on to him and with her petulant jealousy (p. 146). However, his reliance on conventional strategies to persuade Eustacia fail; this proud, supercilious woman has 'mental clearness and power' (p. 148) and a total disregard for public opinion.

Again Hardy's use of striking visual images attracts the reader's attention. The sunlight shining into Eustacia's mouth 'as into a tulip' which 'lent it a similar scarlet fire' (p. 144) is very vivid and this image suggests her vitality and sensuality (with the flaming colour of this spring flower); it also suggests her fiery temper – the 'scarlet fire' of her mouth is redolent of her burning passion and her words which spark with temper and impetuosity.

auroral effects, Polaris in the zenith, Franklin under foot the bird has seen the aurora borealis, a dramatic display of light in the Arctic night sky; Polaris, the North Star at its highest point; and Sir John Franklin (1786–1847) was an English Arctic explorer who disappeared on an Arctic expedition (searches to establish how and where he died were a topic of public discussion during the late 1840s and 1850s)

The great Frederick ... Queen of Prussia during his reign (1740–86) Frederick the Great expanded Prussian power in Europe by exploiting the political weakness of the Archduchess of Austria, Maria Theresa; Napoleon similarly harshly treated the Queen of Prussia after defeating her forces at Jena in 1806

withywind dialect for bindweed or convolvulus which winds itself around other plants

Candaules' wife according to the Greek historian Herodotus (c.484–20BC), the King of Lydia boasted of his wife's beauty and allowed a shepherd, Gyges, to see her naked. Furious, she persuaded Gyges to kill the King and then married him, Gyges then became the King

a Carthaginian bustle ... beauty Carthage is a legendary commercial city in northern Africa, Tarentum was renowned for its luxury, and Baia was a health resort near to Naples; the heath folk perceive Budmouth as a rich, extravagant place of leisure

Zenobia the queen of Palmyra (AD267–272), she expanded her territory by taking advantage of her alliance with Rome

CHAPTER 11   Discovering Venn's love for Thomasin, Mrs Yeobright puts pressure on Wildeve. He then repeats his offer of escape to Eustacia, who realises she does not love him

Venn meets Mrs Yeobright on his way back from Captain Vye's house. He confesses his love for Thomasin and his former proposal. Asserting that it would be better for Thomasin's reputation if she were to marry Wildeve, Mrs Yeobright rejects Venn's renewed offer of marriage. Armed with the news of a rival, she meets with Wildeve to put pressure on him to make a definite commitment to marry her niece. Wildeve then visits Eustacia to obtain a commitment from her to emigrate to America with him. With the sense of competition reduced, Eustacia is forced to admit her real feelings for Wildeve. She will keep him waiting for a week for her answer, however. That evening she discovers that Clym's return from Paris is imminent.

> Venn's confession to Mrs Yeobright sets a chain of events in motion which reveals Wildeve's indifference to Thomasin and Eustacia's sense of shame and folly about her relationship with Wildeve. Both provide a stark contrast with Venn's genuine feelings of love. The **irony** of Eustacia claiming that she is being used as a 'stop-gap' when we can see plainly that it is she who is using Wildeve in this way (as Wildeve is similarly using Thomasin) further emphasises the insincerity and self-centredness of Eustacia and Wildeve and exposes their manipulative behaviour (p. 155). A sense of uncertainty and suspense is created by the indecision of the characters and the different waiting times – Wildeve promises to give Mrs Yeobright his decision in 'a day or two', but this is dependent on Eustacia and she needs a week to give Wildeve her decision (pp. 153, 156). The reader is well aware of what Eustacia's decision will be, especially given her discovery that evening that Clym will soon return.

> Clym's return has been repeatedly referred to, and what we have been told of Eustacia's character, ambitions and longing for a man she can see as an equal make her feelings and behaviour easy to predict. We are left with no doubts about the attraction that this superior man will hold for Eustacia, especially given his association with 'that rookery of pomp and vanity, Paris' (p. 158). A sense of suspense mounts and we are left to speculate at the end of this first book about how this new character will affect the dynamics of the precariously balanced relationship between the characters so far. Reference to Clym's return 'as if it were of national importance' only serves to heighten the anticipation.

BOOK SECOND: THE ARRIVAL

CHAPTER 1   **It is now pubic knowledge that Thomasin and Wildeve**
are not married. Eustacia overhears a conversation
about Clym and later goes to gaze on the Yeobrights'
house

The conversation that Eustacia overhears, as the voices of the furze-cutters Humphrey and Sam and her grandfather travel down the chimney, leads her to consider Clym to be her ideal man. Humphrey and Sam consider that Eustacia and Clym would be compatible in terms of education and social status, and their speculative matchmaking fuels Eustacia's imagination: 'she and Clym Yeobright would make a very pretty pigeon-pair' (p. 163). She spends the afternoon day-dreaming and that evening walks to Blooms-End to gaze at Clym's birthplace.

> It is significant that the discussion of Thomasin's sorry state has no effect on Eustacia; it confirms that Thomasin is no longer a rival since Eustacia no longer wants Wildeve. The prospect of a more suitable match for her in Clym blocks all previous attachments from her mind; he is like 'a man coming from heaven' (p. 164), her dream man, but also suggesting the first man in the Bible, Adam, coming to this barren Eden. The emphasis on how isolated Egdon and its community are builds up a sense of anticipation and prepares us for the immense significance that Clym's return will have. A reminder of Eustacia's age in part explains her excessively romantic dreaming.
>
> The word 'performance' is repeated in this chapter, suggesting again that the novel is like a play unfolding on the stage of Egdon Heath. It is applied to the work of Humphrey and Sam (p. 161) and to Eustacia's visit to Blooms-End (p. 165), and highlights the difference between the two actions – of necessary work and self-indulgence. However, it also suggests some similarity between them – their work and Eustacia's hopes and ambitions are necessary, in different ways, for survival. The idea and language of performance are central to the chapter which deals with the mumming play (Book 2, Chapter 6) and here suggest Eustacia's lack of genuine feeling for Clym from the outset; she is merely following the script she has written for herself and her hero.

pigeon-pair twins of the opposite sex, or a family with a son and a daughter only; the implication is that Eustacia and Clym are a good match because they are similar

scroff dirt

'Castle of Indolence' the long allegorical poem by James Thomson (1700–48) in which the Knight of Art and Industry frees those under the spell of the wizard Indolence

CHAPTER 2   **Thomasin and Mrs Yeobright prepare for Clym's homecoming and discuss Thomasin's marriage to Wildeve**

Whilst Eustacia daydreams of Clym's return, Thomasin and Mrs Yeobright make practical preparations for his homecoming and for Christmas. After picking out the best apples from those stored in the loft, Thomasin goes with her aunt to collect holly from the heath. Their conversation reveals that Thomasin no longer loves Wildeve, but feels compelled to marry him to save her reputation; it also shows her innocence of Wildeve's affair with Eustacia. Mrs Yeobright says that she has tried to prompt Wildeve to renew his offer and disagrees with Thomasin's resolution to keep her trouble a secret from Clym.

Thomasin's sense of shame about her situation is emphasised here as she picks out the apples. This scene alludes to the biblical story of Adam and Eve's fall from Grace as a result of Eve committing the sin of picking the forbidden apple. The adjectives 'lost' (p. 167) and 'fallen' are commonly used in the Victorian period to describe a sexually immoral woman. Thomasin is obviously not to blame, indeed it is Wildeve's immoral behaviour which is prolonging this situation, but her sense of how she will be perceived is very realistic. Her decision to marry Wildeve without loving him, coupled with her innocence of his relationship with Eustacia, adds to the reader's sense of discomfort about this union.

The action of this 'scene' takes place at the same time as that of the previous chapter and we are seemingly invited to make comparisons between the three women. The imagery and associations used to describe Thomasin and Eustacia stress the differences between them. A contrast between pastoral and mythic allusion effectively highlights these differences: Thomasin is described as a 'maiden' whose innocent sensuality as she 'plunged her naked arms into the soft brown fern' (p. 166) contrasts with the description of Eustacia which associates her with goddesses and a conscious awareness of her passions. Most striking is the contrast using imagery of light and darkness. As we have already seen Eustacia is associated with darkness and night whereas the sunlight almost seems to shine through Thomasin as it illuminates her fair hair and complexion (see Characterisation). There are similarities drawn between Eustacia and Mrs Yeobright (here and throughout the novel), however; both are proud and superior, a similarity which will soon lead to a clash between them.

Thomasin's reason for not wanting to 'pain' Clym with the news of her situation 'since he loved me once' is ambiguous and suggests a romantic rather than a familial love; the allusions to the biblical myth of Adam and Eve in this and the previous chapter add to this suggestion.

russets … ribstones varieties of apple

CHAPTER 3 **Eustacia's patience is rewarded when Clym speaks to her; her state of nervous excitement causes her to have a strange dream. She looks for him on the heath for the next five days, but is disappointed**

Eustacia has watched for Clym's arrival, but it is as she is disappointedly returning home that Clym, Thomasin and Mrs Yeobright pass her. Clym's polite and customary 'Goodnight!' sets her imagination whirling. Eustacia returns home in a state of nervous excitement. Her conversation with her grandfather reveals that the Yeobrights are as genteel as she may wish and Captain Vye attributes the unfriendliness between the families to his accidentally offending Mrs Yeobright. Eustacia's dream that night is wild and vivid, complex, confusing and prophetic. Her hope of meeting Clym on the heath is frustrated, but a meeting is imminent.

Eustacia's impression of Clym at this point is almost entirely a projection of her own needs and desires; in her dream he is a somewhat clichéd knight in shining armour. However, the scenario she so vividly imagines is also prophetic of her relationships with both of her lovers: it anticipates her first meeting with Clym, where the roles are reversed and Eustacia plays the heathen knight, her dance with Wildeve as her marriage with Clym breaks down, and ultimately her death in the pool with Wildeve. The fact that her knight 'fell into fragments' is ominous and that she never sees his face predicts how she will never really know and understand Clym. Indeed, her twice repeated puzzlement about Clym's love of the landscape demonstrates this incomprehension of Clym from the outset of their relationship (p. 172). Her dream also foretells how her self-created romantic illusions about him will be shattered. The lack of a fixed identity for her lover suggests that her hero could be any man who can enable her to escape the heath which appears 'dimly' as the backdrop to her fantasy and haunts 'the brilliancy of the action' (pp. 173–4).

Dr Kitto a well-known deaf biblical scholar (1804–54) who wrote *The Lost Senses*
Nebuchadnezzar the King of Babylon who dreamed elaborate dreams
Swaffham tinker John Bunyan whose famous book, *The Pilgrim's Progress*, is based on his remarkable dreams
Cretan labyrinth in Greek myth this was the complex labyrinth where the minotaur (half bull half man) was kept
Queen Scheherazade the narrator in *The Arabian Nights* who escaped death only by telling her husband stories to stop him from killing her

CHAPTER 4   **Eustacia persuades Charley to let her take his part in the mumming play at Mrs Yeobright's house**

Just as Eustacia's hopes of meeting Clym before he returns to the 'gay city' of Paris are disappearing, an opportunity arises which allows her to contrive to see him. Spying on the mummers as they practise in the fuel-house, Eustacia overhears them discussing their first performance at Mrs Yeobright's party. Her disappointment at missing out on an opportunity to see Clym leads her to create one for herself. When Charley returns the key she strikes a bargain with him; she will play his part of the Turkish Knight at Mrs Yeobright's and he will be allowed to hold her hand and kiss it. The following evening Charley returns with his costume and watches Eustacia perform his part. He claims his part of the bargain, but is full of regret when the time runs out.

Again the Egdon community's lack of Christian faith is made apparent in their attitude to churchgoing and Christmas. A cynical attitude to orthodox religion is also evident in the fact that, although the mumming play depicts a battle between Christianity and paganism, in this performance there is no distinction between the Christians and the heathens (p. 179). The continuation of mumming plays as a 'traditional pastime' blends and confuses the two modes of belief. Again the heath folk are treated somewhat comically and the sartorial battles of the players' sweethearts, which ends in ridiculous costumes, is far more serious than the moral struggle that the play of St George enacts. Hardy also seems to be making an important point about good and evil; his blurring of the distinctions between **symbolic** figures who are supposed to clearly represent good or evil seems to be a warning to the reader about making facile moral judgements about his characters. They are complex and not to be reductively categorised.

Tussaud Madame Tussaud's exhibition was established in London in 1835 and contains life-size wax replicas of famous figures, including a criminal gallery
Balaam the prophet in the Bible who tried to go against God but was forced to say what God ordered him to
unweeting automatic, unthinking
the well-known play of 'St George' the mumming plays developed from pagan festivities which celebrated the conflict between summer and winter; in the Christian play St George (the patron saint of England) took the place of Summer, and Saladin took the place of Winter. Hardy often saw this play performed at village festivals and assisted in restoring the text of the play which was published in 1928
Gorget … visor armour and clothing for various parts of the body
Raffaelle after Perugino Raphaelo Santi (the Italian painter 1483–1520) was the pupil of Pietro Vannuci (Perugino) (1481–1537); his paintings were considered by the Victorians to be superior to those of his teacher, suggesting that Eustacia is a better performer than Charley

CHAPTER 5   **The mummers enact their play at Mrs Yeobright's house**

Initially posing as her cousin, Eustacia persuades the players that she is able to perform Charley's part. As they wait outside Mrs Yeobright's house for the dancing to stop, the others guess her real identity but promise to keep it secret. Once inside and performing the play Eustacia has little time to look for Clym until she has been slain and, managing to keep her head elevated, she searches the room for him.

> The discussion about time again adds a note of comedy to the activities and lives of the heath folk but, as we have seen in the previous chapter, such apparently patronising depictions of rustic characters actually express more serious philosophical concerns. With this mention of time we are reminded of the power that the heath seems to exert over time on any scale – historical, geological, mythological – and here time takes on an almost religious significance, its measurement being bound up with 'doctrines', 'faiths', 'tenets', 'followers' and beliefs (p. 186). This is possibly an allusion to how a concern with time, particularly evolutionary time, has supplanted religious belief in Hardy's contemporary society (see Narrative Techniques and Historical Background).

the serpent an obsolete wind instrument

CHAPTER 6   **Eustacia sees Clym and his curiosity about her is aroused; he guesses that she is woman. As she walks home she remembers her appointment with Wildeve, but only wishes now that he had married Thomasin**

Eustacia has gone to the Yeobrights' house in search of a 'hero' (p. 187) and the effect on Eustacia of seeing Clym is great, 'palpable' (p. 195). After the play Grandfer Cantle, Christian and Fairway enter and Fairway expresses his admiration for Clym, whilst Grandfer Cantle boasts of his own good looks in the past and of his youthful spirit now, and Christian expresses his fears and superstitions. The party sit down to eat and drink and Clym's curiosity is aroused when Eustacia refuses to eat. His affectionate exchange with Thomasin once again fills Eustacia with burning jealousy for Thomasin and she guesses that Clym does not know of Thomasin's predicament. Feeling very uneasy, Eustacia goes outside. Clym follows her and asks whether she is a woman; he is curious about her motives but does not pry. She refuses to go back inside and now 'warmed with an inner fire' she sets off for home through the frosty night (p. 202). She remembers that she promised to give Wildeve an answer to his proposal, but is only angry with herself now for stopping him from marrying Thomasin.

Clym's appearance is highly significant; he is described as a young, attractive man whose features have been distorted by the intensity of his mental activity: 'an inner strenuousness was preying upon an outer symmetry' giving him a 'singular' look (p. 194). He has the face of a 'modern man' whose intellectual striving for understanding is draining him of classical beauty and natural vitality. He does have a god-like quality which shines like a ray out of the 'carcase' of his body (p. 195). Although this reference in no way compares with the excessive description of Eustacia's 'divinity', their location outside the settle does symbolically suggest some connection between them. Compared to a line of trees which ameliorates the effects of harsh nature, the settle encloses those within it in a 'Paradise' free of draughts (p. 193); Clym and Eustacia, however, are both outside of such communal social space and comfort. They are both in different ways cut off from this close community of ordinary people, a factor which draws them together and which ultimately contributes to their **tragedy**.

'Nancy's Fancy' a dance where men and women stand in a line facing each other

'Devil's Dream' a six-handed reel, also known as 'The Devil Among the Tailors'

Rembrandt Rembrandt van Rijn (1606–69) was a Dutch painter whose work attempted to convey the inner moods of his subjects by use of contrasts of dark and light and rich colours; he frequently painted ordinary domestic scenes and biblical subjects

Jared, Mahalaleel, and the rest of the antediluvians biblical figures who lived long lives before the Flood; Jared lived until he was 962 years old, his father, Mahalaleel, until he was 895, and Methusaleh until he was 969 (Genesis 5)

scammish untidy, clumsy

Boney Bonaparte

bagnet bayonet

spatter-dashes leggings to protect clothing from being spattered

Queen of Love appeared before Aeneas in Virgil's Aeneid, Aeneas' mother, Venus, appears to her son in disguise, but he does not recognise her until just before she disappears

Echo in Greek mythology the nymph Echo was in love with Narcissus, but she could only repeat the last words spoken by others; Narcissus was so in love with his own reflection that he did not notice her

Polly Peachum a character in John Gay's *The Beggar's Opera* (1728); the first actress to play this role, Lavinia Fenton (1708–60), married the Duke of Bolton

Lydia Languish a character in Richard Sheridan's *The Rivals* (1775); the actress, Elizabeth Farren, who played this role married the first Earl of Derby in 1797

CHAPTER 7   **Eustacia sends a letter to Wildeve; Wildeve sets a date for his marriage to Thomasin, and Venn's hopes are dashed once again**

Eustacia confesses her escapade to her grandfather and shortly afterwards Venn approaches her. She is now keen to see Wildeve marry Thomasin and, having avoided Wildeve by hiding in Venn's van, she writes a letter which ends her relationship with him. Venn delivers it to Wildeve that night when he is waiting again for Eustacia at Rainbarrow. Wildeve wonders at Venn acting against his own interests and tells him what Mrs Yeobright had said about his being a rival suitor for Thomasin's hand. With cruel resolve to marry Thomasin quickly in order to punish Eustacia, Wildeve sets off for Blooms-End. Venn too, full of renewed hope, sets off for his van. In the time it takes for him to dress himself in a way which will gain approval, however, Wildeve has been accepted. Just as Venn arrives at the Yeobrights' house, Wildeve emerges triumphant. After a short conversation with Mrs Yeobright, Venn returns to his van in utter despondency and resumes the clothes of the reddleman; these now clearly express his sense of rejection and pain.

What we know to be only Mrs Yeobright's ruse causes Venn real and undeserved pain here. The question of whether he would have been perceived as acceptable by Mrs Yeobright, even in his best clothes and prepared to give up his trade, however, is raised by the way that she does not invite him into her home. Once again Venn's selfless love and actions contrast sharply with those of Eustacia, Wildeve and Mrs Yeobright; both Eustacia and Wildeve express their total lack of understanding of his sense of duty.

Ahasuerus the Jew the legendary Wandering Jew condemned to roam the earth until Jesus' second coming as a punishment for striking Christ as he carried his cross

Zin in the Bible this was the wilderness through which the Israelites wandered on their journey to the Promised Land (Numbers 33:6)

pis aller meaning what is accepted when there is nothing better

like Satan at the touch of Ithuriel's spear in John Milton's *Paradise Lost* (1667), when the angel Ithuriel discovers Satan tempting Eve in a dream, he returns him to his true shape by touching him with his spear

CHAPTER 8   **Thomasin and Wildeve finally marry; Venn observes the wedding and tells Clym and his mother about Eustacia's involvement in it**

After Wildeve has left, Thomasin and her aunt discuss the wedding. Thomasin's resolve to 'marry him under any circumstances' has been strengthened by a letter from Clym who is shocked by the rumours he has heard, whilst visiting a friend, of Thomasin being jilted. Venn's call prompts Thomasin to expresses her pity for him. She and her aunt have a busy day preparing for her wedding and Thomasin declines Mrs Yeobright's offer to give her away. She sets off for church the following day, alone and uncertain. Clym returns and is angry about not being told of Thomasin's marriage in the first place; his previous romantic attachment to Thomasin, which has been hinted at previously, is revealed, as is Mrs Yeobright's bitterness about Thomasin's lack of mutual affection for Clym. He sets out to go to the wedding, but returns shortly afterwards with Venn who reports that the marriage has taken place and that Eustacia, her identity hidden by a thick veil, gave Thomasin away. He did not reveal Wildeve's obvious shock and anger when Eustacia lifted the veil to sign the register, nor that his and Eustacia's attendance was planned and not coincidental. We are also told of what Venn did not see and hear – the bitter exchange in looks and words which passed between Wildeve and Eustacia. After this Venn 'vanished entirely', not returning to the heath for many months (p. 221).

> Clym's unexplained regret about Mrs Yeobright's party again alerts us to the probable development of a relationship between Eustacia and Clym. We see Mrs Yeobright's tendency to hold bitter grudges when people do not behave as she wants them to (as towards Thomasin because she thwarted her plan for a union between her niece and her son). In the light of this tendency, Clym's choice of a woman of whom his mother will inevitably disapprove does not bode well. Wildeve and Thomasin's marriage ceremony, as with that of Eustacia and Clym, takes place 'off-stage' and is described by report. Given the heath folk's criticisms of the antisocial nature of private celebrations, there is a sense that from the outset these unions are destined to fail since they are not in harmony with communal life on the heath.

gypsyings open-air village festivals

BOOK THIRD: THE FASCINATION

CHAPTER 1   **Clym announces his plans to set up a school at Fairway's regular Sunday hair-cutting**

Again Clym is identified as a modern man and his face reflects 'the quandary' of modern life, disillusionment and the recognition of 'the defects of natural laws' (p. 225). His reputation from a young age has been of someone who would break away from the life on the heath and do something out of the ordinary with equal chance of success or failure. Paradoxically, he is also integrally connected to the heath and its community. Clym tells the heath men his plans, but when he has gone they express their doubts about whether he will stay and voice some hostility at what they perceive as his interference in their way of life.

There is some emphasis placed on the manly and courteous behaviour of the heath men as they endure the stabs from the scissors and, despite the great difference in experience and ideas, Clym is like them. He wants to give up the 'effeminate' diamond business in order to play an integral role in this community (as is confirmed in the following chapter). Fairway speaks with 'a tone of integrity' and Clym's aims express his integrity and his 'earnestness' (p. 228). However, although motivated by a genuine desire to improve the lives of the heath folk, Clym's plans suggest a real lack of understanding of their lives and values. The emphasis on his modernity and his awareness of ideas generated in Paris stress his alienation from his place of origin and the traditional ways of life. Hardy seems to be suggesting that Clym's progressive and reforming ideas are not inherently wrong, but that they clash with the traditions on the heath.

'My mind to Me a Kingdom is' the first line of a poem about contentment with intellectual achievement, commonly attributed to Edward Dyer (1550–1607) and first published in William Byrd's *Psalmes, Sonets, and Songs* (1588)

Pheidias a great sculptor (*c.*490–432BC) who supervised the building of the Parthenon in Athens; his famous sculptures of Zeus and Athena are said to be the initiators of the classical Greek style

Aeschylus the Greek dramatist (525–456BC) who wrote many tragedies

Spanish Jesuit Gracian Balthasar Gracian y Morales (1601–58), the Spanish churchman and writer

Homer the ancient Greek poet (who probably lived between 1100–900BC) is said to have written the *Illiad* and the *Odyssey*

Clive Robert Clive (1725–74), began as a clerk and became the British commander in India and is considered to be the founder of the British Empire in India

Gay John Gay (1685–1732), began as a draper's apprentice and became a poet and playwright; author of *The Beggar's Opera*

Keats John Keats (1795–1821) studied to become a surgeon but became a Romantic poet

mollyhorning idling and wasting time

CHAPTER 2   **Clym tells his mother his plans. Christian reports the pricking of Eustacia in church, and Sam comes to borrow a rope to retrieve Captain Vye's bucket from his well**

Clym's expectation of his mother's disapproval of this plans to give up his business and become a teacher of the poor is confirmed. She cannot comprehend such 'going backward in the world' out of choice (p. 233). Clym tells her he has spent a long time agonising over his decision, and wants to 'do some worthy thing' with his life (p. 233). Their discussion is interrupted by Christian who reports that Susan Nunsuch has pricked Eustacia with a stocking needle in order to end the spell that she thinks Eustacia has cast on her children; Clym uses this proof of the need for education to strengthen his argument. Sam arrives to borrow a rope and Mrs Yeobright tries to put a stop to Clym's obvious interest in 'the beauty on the hill' (p. 236). Sam suggests that Clym could see her if he came to help to retrieve Captain Vye's well bucket that evening.

> Mrs Yeobright is angry with Clym for what she sees as his lack of ambition; it clearly undermines her vicarious sense of success. Her attempt to stifle his interest in Eustacia stems from a strong disapproval of her. Later when Clym and Eustacia's relationship is developing, the reader's knowledge of Mrs Yeobright's feeling about Eustacia helps to create a sense of uneasy tension. At this point, however, Clym's interest in her is largely practical; if Eustacia was the mummer, he realises that she could be of use in his teaching plans. Although Clym and his mother are at odds here, their relationship is very close (as explicit comments in the following chapter show); the evolutionary language, 'inherited … instincts', also stresses this closeness (p. 234). It is important to recognise that their love for each other is very deep in order to appreciate the tremendous impact caused by their estrangement over Clym's relationship with Eustacia.

> Clym's project, influenced by the ideas of the French Utopian socialists of the 1840s, is well-intentioned, but its inappropriateness and inevitable failure are spelt out very clearly in this chapter. It is too far in advance of the ideas and stage of development of the

heath folk, and it disrupts the customary sequence of cultural advancement from rustic, through material and social gains, to intellectual development. Hardy moved in intellectual London circles and was well aware of the ideas for improvement of the quality of human life circulating in the mid-late nineteenth century. However, he was also aware of the inappropriateness of imposing metropolitan ideals onto a rural community such as the one he depicts in this novel. Although Clym's ideas are consistent with those of 'the central town thinkers of his date', '[t]he rural world was not ripe for him' (p. 230).

John the Baptist in the Bible, he preceded Christ and asked people to repent (Matthew 3:3)

ethical systems suggests that Clym is influenced by Auguste Comte's humanist theory of Positivism

Chaldeans the ancient Babylonian practitioners of astronomy and astrology

Rogers ... Tomline were all famous although their work was considered mediocre. Samuel Rogers (1763–1855) was a poet, popular in his lifetime but quickly forgotten after his death; Benjamin West (1738–1820) was an American painter who became popular in London; Lord North (1732–92) an unsuccessful statesman who acted as Prime Minister of Britain during the American War of Independence; Sir George Tomline (1750–1827) was Bishop of Winchester, but was complacent in his attitudes

CHAPTER 3   Clym goes to Captain Vye's and talks to Eustacia. As their relationship develops, Clym's relationship with his mother becomes increasingly fraught

After walking with his mother on the heath that afternoon, Clym sets off for Captain Vye's house. The heath men and Clym successfully retrieve the bucket, but it has a hole in it and water cannot be drawn. The pool water is drinkable, but Eustacia refuses to drink it; she is injured for the second time that day as she helps Clym to get water from the well using a pail. She shows him her stocking needle wound and Clym asks whether she would help him to end such superstitious beliefs by teaching. Eustacia is not interested in such work but offers to listen to his plans. Clym feels as if he has reached a turning point but, as his relationship with Eustacia develops, his relationship with his mother rapidly deteriorates. Mrs Yeobright's jealousy is evident and she vents her bitter resentment and disapproval of Eustacia. Clym modifies his plans, ostensibly to satisfy his mother's ambitions, though possibly also to try to entice Eustacia to become involved. Mrs Yeobright warns him that he is very mistaken, 'blinded', in his judgement of Eustacia (p. 252); Clym leaves the house and returns late that night.

> Once again Christian's obsession with superstition (as in the previous chapter) leads him to bring news (of the urn Clym has given to Eustacia) which stirs Mrs Yeobright's anger and further disrupts the bond between mother and son. Later his superstition about the dice contributes significantly to the development of the **tragedy**. **Dramatic irony** is used to highlight the similarities between Eustacia and Mrs Yeobright: Mrs Yeobright blames Eustacia for Clym's continuing determination to teach; however, Eustacia's real ambitions very much resemble Mrs Yeobright's.
>
> Both Clym and Eustacia feel inspired by their meeting at the well, and both feel that their dreams can now be realised; their dreams are in direct conflict, however, as their attitudes to the heath and to the heath folk reveal. Attitudes to the heath act as a gauge of character, as well as repeatedly signalling the incompatibility of Eustacia and Clym. The **imagery** used in this chapter is very revealing and anticipates the future for the new lovers. As Eustacia shows Clym the pool and mimics the signal for her secret meetings with Wildeve, ideas of romance are suggested, as is the idea of new life that water often symbolises. However, the gruesome **simile** used to describe the pool, 'an eye without its pupil' (p. 242), undermines any ideas that this relationship will be successful. The pool's blindness suggests that Clym and Eustacia do not see each other clearly (as Mrs Yeobright also warns Clym). As spring and their relationship advance, the pool comes to life but, significantly, Clym, who is usually in tune with the heath and its natural cycles, does not notice. In the following chapter, the moon imagery similarly adds an ominous note to Eustacia's acceptance of Clym's marriage proposal.

well-roller pulley
Druidical stone used by the ancient order of priests, the Druids, in their rites

crochets odd ideas, whims

Blacklock Thomas Blacklock (1721–91) was a Scottish divine and poet who became blind at six months old as a result of smallpox

Sanderson Nicholas Sanderson (1682–1739) was Professor of Mathematics at Cambridge who became blind at the age of one, also as a result of smallpox

Sallaert, Van Alsloot Anthony Sallaert (1590–c.1648) and Denis van Alsloot were Flemish painters who often painted large groups of people, thus requiring them to look at society from a distance

CHAPTER 4   **Clym proposes to Eustacia on Rainbarrow and returns home fully aware of the dilemma he is now in**

Clym waits for Eustacia on Rainbarrow. As the moon's eclipse begins, Eustacia arrives and **melodramatically** expresses her pessimism about the endurance of Clym's love for her, especially because of his mother's influence. Their discussion reveals that their hopes for the future clash completely, but, despite this, Clym pursues his proposal and Eustacia, seeing that Clym seems to be reconsidering a relationship with 'one whose tastes only touched his at rare and infrequent points', accepts him (p. 258). They return to Mistover; Eustacia will speak to her grandfather about their marriage. As Clym returns home, his recognition that Eustacia is attracted to him as 'a visitant from a gay world' who could take her back there makes him doubtful of the success of their marriage (p. 259). His turmoil over the breach with his mother and how this will be exacerbated by his marriage makes him realise the impossible situation he is in. He acknowledges that 'his mother's trust in him, his plan for becoming a teacher, and Eustacia's happiness' cannot all be 'kept alive' (p. 260).

> The moon is used to represent the different aspirations of Clym and Eustacia. As he gazes at it before Eustacia arrives, Clym imagines that it is his ideal world 'where personal progress was not the only recognised form of progress' (p. 254). In contrast, for Eustacia the moon shining on Clym's face means he 'should be doing better things' (p. 258). The fact that it is eclipsed has negative implications for the future and their dreams. Eustacia's repeated reference to the failure of love to last is an aspect of her melodramatic

romanticism, but accurately predicts the transience of her love for Clym. Their dialogue is full of foreboding.

We also see that, despite the conflict between mother and son, Clym's love for his mother is deep. The final line of the chapter generates a change in our assessment of Mrs Yeobright and an element of concern creeps in; her physical distress when she hears of his marriage to Eustacia in the following chapter adds to this concern (p. 262).

Bay of Rainbows ... Ring Mountains imaginary names for areas on the moon's surface

Tuileries a former royal palace in Paris

Louvre art gallery in Paris

Versailles the site of Louis XIV's palace and gardens

Trianon the small palace built in Versailles

Fontainbleau the site of Louis IX's palace and gardens north of Paris

St Cloud the royal chateau near Paris which was destroyed during the Franco-Prussian war

the Bois the park on the edge of Paris

Petrarch ... Laura the Italian lyric poet and humanist (1304–74), was inspired to write poems about his love for Laura, whom he saw but never met

CHAPTER 5   **Mrs Yeobright hears that Clym and Eustacia are engaged; Clym meets Eustacia and they set a date for their wedding**

Mrs Yeobright is obviously 'shaken' and angered by the news of Clym's marriage, received not from Clym, but via Captain Vye's gossip in the Quiet Woman. She criticises Eustacia harshly and complains bitterly that Clym puts Eustacia before her. As the tension mounts, Clym declares he will leave home. He had planned that his mother and Eustacia should meet that day, but he goes out to meet Eustacia alone. From the outside they look like a perfect couple, forming 'a very comely picture of love at full flush', but Eustacia's sense of triumph at 'having won' a man who is 'her perfect complement in attainments, appearance, and age' is clouded by her fear of Mrs Yeobright's influence (p. 265). Partly as a reaction against his mother's wishes, and partly as a reaction to the romantic setting, Clym proposes that they marry immediately and live secluded in a small cottage for six months until he is ready to open his school in Budmouth. Eustacia agrees to marry him in two weeks time. They part and, as he watches Eustacia's retreating figure, Clym once again feels some sense of regret about the development of their relationship.

> The scene of Clym and Eustacia's meeting is a typically romantic one; the sunset draws out beautiful colours and creates a 'purple haze' which seems to heighten Clym's passion. Indirectly, it also reveals both the intensity and the fragility of their love which, like the sunset, is powerful but transitory. As Eustacia 'retired towards the sun', the intoxication that Clym felt in her presence dies down and at 'a cooler moment' he regrets his haste in setting a date (p. 267). However, he has taken his chance and, like Eustacia, he now puts his future in the hands of fate. Summer is symbolically the time of intensity, vitality and passion, but Clym's sense of being 'overpowered' and oppressed by the 'horizontality' (p. 267) of the heath in its full summer greenery, and his sense of being somehow in a state of suspended time amidst 'machine-made foliage' (p. 264) sounds an ominous note. It suggests a state of disharmony with nature and the heath. His sense that the scene 'seemed to belong to the ancient world of the carboniferous period' where 'no bird sang' accurately builds a sense of the hush of a summer's day, but, in the light of the evolutionary theory which underlies the novel, it also suggests a regression and Clym's discord with natural cycles and with human progression. This sense of discord with nature is also suggested by the weather in the following chapter.

carboniferous period began 350 million years ago

CHAPTER 6   **Clym leaves home. Thomasin visits Mrs Yeobright to comfort her, and Wildeve's desire for Eustacia is renewed by the news of her imminent marriage to Clym**

The following day, despite an unseasonable violent storm, Clym sets off to rent a house six miles away that he considers to be suitably secluded. The next day he sends his things to his rented cottage and goes to buy some furniture at Angelbury. Clym tells his mother the date of his wedding and she says it is unlikely that she will visit them. Clym is intensely upset and Mrs Yeobright is numbed with the shock of his departure. Hearing of Clym's departure, Thomasin visits her aunt to try to comfort her. Mrs Yeobright finally expresses her grief, but refuses to see the unreasonableness of her attitude to Clym's ambitions, which she considers the 'wrong' course. In the heat of her anger, she disowns him. Thomasin is anxious about asking Wildeve for money; Mrs Yeobright reminds Thomasin of the inheritance she is keeping for her, but advises her to ask Wildeve for money first. When Wildeve discovers that Eustacia is about to be married he immediately longs for her again.

> The violent storm in which Clym sets out contributes to our mounting sense of foreboding (and his sense of doubt) about his decision to marry Eustacia; winter, symbolically the death of the year, completely dashes the hope associated with summer. Its brutal effect on the young trees, which are specifically associated with Clym, is particularly effective as the pain and damage is described in terms usually applied to the human body: 'amputations, bruises, cripplings, and harsh lacerations, from which the wasting sap would bleed for many a day to come, and which would leave scars visible till the day of their burning' (p. 268). This **imagery** predicts Clym's future: although his physical pain will not be so great as this dramatic description suggests, his psychological suffering matches the agonies so vividly attributed to the beech trees. Like their physical scars, his emotional scars will last until his death.
>
> Already there seems to be problems in Thomasin's marriage to Wildeve, and the reader is made aware that Wildeve's renewed desire for Eustacia will probably jeopardise this relationship further. We are encouraged to have an ambiguous response to Mrs Yeobright in this chapter: while we, like Thomasin, condemn her narrow-mined inflexibility, we have some sympathy for her pain and loneliness now that she has lost her only son in whom she had invested so much of herself.

spade-guineas guineas minted in the late eighteenth century with a spade imprinted on them

Ulysses the hero of Homer's *Odyssey*

stun-poll like a fool, stunned by Eustacia's beauty

Rousseau Jean Jacques Rousseau (1712–78) was a leading French humanist philosopher whose principles and conduct were unorthodox

CHAPTER 7   It is Clym and Eustacia's wedding day and Mrs Yeobright decides to send Thomasin's and Clym's inheritance money to them at Mistover via Christian. Feeling lucky he gambles and loses all one hundred guineas to Wildeve

Although Mrs Yeobright has declined to go to the wedding, she is preoccupied with the event. Thomasin had been due to collect her inheritance money but, because she had been pressed to go to the wedding, Wildeve calls instead. However, Mrs Yeobright does not trust him with the money. She decides to send Thomasin's and Clym's money to Mistover Knap with Christian; this will prevent Wildeve from discovering Thomasin's inheritance, and will be a sign of goodwill to Clym. Christian is distracted from his errand by the raffle at the Quiet Woman, which he wins. He reveals to Wildeve that he has something to give to Thomasin and they set off for Mistover together. Guessing that Christian has money for Thomasin, Wildeve is affronted at Mrs Yeobright's distrust of him and for revenge decides to win it from Christian, who is obsessed with the dice and his luck. Inevitably Christian loses not only Thomasin's money but also Clym's. Exhausted, Christian leaves and Venn, who had seen Wildeve and Christian leave the inn, approaches Wildeve.

> Once again we see how Christian's superstition, foolishness and obsessiveness contributes directly to the sequence of tragic events; Venn will attempt to restore harmony but, not equipped with all the facts (that half of the money is Clym's), also unwittingly contributes to the tragedy. The antagonism between Wildeve and Mrs Yeobright, however, is also a significant factor initially motivating Wildeve to gamble with Christian, though his personal greed quickly becomes the driving force of his actions. Wildeve uses his control over money to assert his superiority over Christian here, as it is hinted he does in his relationship with Thomasin as well.

Pitt Diamond Thomas Pitt (1653–1726) was governor of Madras; he sent a
large diamond to England, reputedly hidden in the sole of a shoe
ba'dy gaities bawdy stories or indecent remarks
born w' a caul a caul is the amniotic sack which sometimes remains after
birth, it is said to be lucky
chips-in-porridge an insignificant or useless person

CHAPTER 8   **Venn wins back the money from Wildeve, but
mistakenly gives it all to Thomasin as she returns from
Clym and Eustacia's wedding**

Carried away with the excitement of winning, Wildeve accepts Venn's
challenge and continues to gamble. Venn's aim is to right the wrong done
to Thomasin and Mrs Yeobright and the stone on which they gamble
becomes a 'battle-field' (p. 290). Venn's calm impassive disposition
(seemingly inhuman, as he is likened twice to an 'automaton' and also to
'a red-sandstone statue') contrasts dramatically with Wildeve's
increasingly nervous excitability as Venn triumphs over him, taunting
him with the story Wildeve used to encourage Christian to gamble.
When he has won it all, Venn gathers the money and leaves Wildeve
momentarily stupified. Walking home, however, Wildeve sees Eustacia
and Clym's carriage pass and the loss of the money pales into
insignificance 'at the sight if his lost love' (p. 294). Venn, further down
the road than Wildeve, stops the carriage and having discovered that
Thomasin is in the following carriage, he waits and gives all of the money
to her. Venn returns to his van and falls into an exhausted sleep.

In this episode Hardy builds up a tightly-controlled sense of
suspense. There is a pattern of mounting tension, as Wildeve loses
and becomes increasingly frantic and reckless, which is then broken
at several points by interruptions to their game. This suspense holds
the reader's attention until the final game when Wildeve feels as if
his luck has turned, but finds that his 'sheer rage' earlier has caused
the die to split and Venn has won. Their actions are at odds with
the natural setting, and it is heath creatures which interrupt the
game; the heath-croppers' curiosity and the death's head moth
both cause the game to be suspended. This suggests that, although
humans may try to interfere with destiny, their actions will

ultimately not affect the mysterious forces operating on the heath which seem to have ultimate control of events. Indeed, the characters here think that they are merely playing at dice; they have no knowledge of what the stakes really are. The flat stone becomes the focus of attention for all of them; its description as another world ('the flat stone ... the whole world to them', p. 286, and 'the little flat stone, which to them was an arena vast and important' – p. 290) hints that like the game, their world is subject to chance which no one can alter. The magical number of glowworms are used for a purely practical purpose, but also add to the atmosphere; the number thirteen is traditionally associated with bad luck, and Venn's success in this light certainly adds to the tragic events.

The title of this book, 'The Fascination', is a significant one and fascination and obsession have featured prominently in the development of events so far and will continue to do so. The new dawn which ends this chapter seems to bode well, but this is undermined by the narrative warning about the trouble which Venn's error will cause.

heath-croppers   wild ponies

BOOK FOURTH: THE CLOSED DOOR

CHAPTER 1   **Wondering whether her gift has reached Clym, Mrs Yeobright goes to meet Eustacia; an initial misunderstanding gives rise to expressions of anger and regret on both sides**

For the first few weeks Clym and Eustacia live a blissful existence; it is the height of summer and their seclusion intensifies the romance. When Clym resumes his study, Eustacia begins to doubt that she will be able to convince Clym to return to Paris. Although she has received thanks for her gift from Thomasin, Mrs Yeobright is anxious because she has heard nothing from Clym. She takes the opportunity of Eustacia's visit to her grandfather to ask whether her gift had been received. Christian confesses his gambling and Mrs Yeobright, although painfully irritated, thinks it likely that Wildeve would have passed on the money to Eustacia.

Meeting Eustacia at the pool, Mrs Yeobright's question about the receipt of the money from Wildeve sparks a vehement exchange, which reveals Eustacia's sense of superiority to the Yeobrights, her bitter regret that Clym will not return to Paris, and her anger at Mrs Yeobright's attempts to deter Clym from marrying her. Mrs Yeobright's angry passion, pride and bitterness are a match for Eustacia's and she warns that Clym can be hard.

Here we see the similarities between Mrs Yeobright and Eustacia very clearly. As their argument progresses our sympathy shifts towards Mrs Yeobright, who is now trying to make amends by welcoming Eustacia and by sending her 'sacred gift' to try to heal the rift with her son. Eustacia's accusation that Mrs Yeobright has 'caused a division which can never be healed' (p. 304) is **ironic** in this context, since it is Eustacia who is maintaining that rift (as she unintentionally does later). As Eustacia returns repeatedly to what she suspects is Mrs Yeobright's knowledge of her involvement with Wildeve, we realise that her outburst is at least partly motivated by a guilty defensiveness about her past and her reputation. Mrs Yeobright is referred to with three anonymous terms, the 'mother-in-law', 'the visitor' and the 'excited mother', which denote the shifts in her relationship to Eustacia and Clym. When she first approaches Eustacia she is referred to as 'mother-in-law', suggesting her intention of improving her connection with her daughter-in-law. However, Eustacia's cold response puts this in jeopardy and identifies Mrs Yeobright as merely a 'visitor' not a relative. By the end of the chapter she is again referred to as 'mother', any connection she attempted to forge with Eustacia having been thwarted by Eustacia's harsh criticism of what Mrs Yeobright sees as her dutiful behaviour as a mother.

References to time occur frequently in this book and add to the sense of mounting tension. The fact that the whole year is described in diurnal terms creates a sense that the year will pass as rapidly as a day as the novel speeds towards the tragic outcome.

CHAPTER 2   In studying hard in order to achieve his goals more
quickly, Clym temporarily damages his eyesight.
Eustacia despairs of leaving the heath when he takes up
furze-cutting and the rift between them widens

Clym's hopes of reconciliation are shattered when Eustacia tells him of
her meeting with his mother. He is surprised when she uses this incident
to urge him to take her to Paris, and this makes him determined to
achieve his goals of opening a school in Budmouth more quickly.
Thomasin brings Clym's share of the guineas the following day and
informs him of his mother's distraught state. Acute inflammation of the
eyes caused by extensive reading leads to Clym's vision being temporarily
impaired, a situation which causes Eustacia to be anxious about his failure
and her entrapment in such a humble life. Described as 'an absolute stoic
in the face of mishaps which only affected his social standing' Clym
decides to earn a living as a furze-cutter, to Eustacia's complete
humiliation (p. 310). Hearing him sing as he works one day, Eustacia's
sense of injured pride causes her to implicitly express her anger and regret
at marrying him; she admits that her love, after only two months, is
'cooling' (p. 315). Clym asserts that his experience of life prevents him
from feeling the ignominy that Eustacia feels; she walks home in tears.

Clym's literal loss of eyesight **symbolises** his blindness in his
judgement of Eustacia and of his educational scheme. As Clym
works on the heath he is once more in complete harmony with its
colours and creatures. This not only serves to highlight the
widening gulf between Clym and Eustacia, but also suggests his
insignificance in this universe and the dissipation of his
modernising impulse in the face of such a place. For Eustacia to see
him working, 'a brown spot in the midst of an expanse of olive-
green gorse, and nothing more', brings home forcefully the fact that
he is not the hero who will enable her to escape the heath (p. 312).

'Rasselas' in this novel written by Samuel Johnson (1709–84), Rasselas
tries to escape from the Happy Valley by means of wings made by an
inventor; he fails to fly but escapes by other means
'Le point du jour' a French song about a shepherd's pain at leaving his loved
one at daybreak

CHAPTER 3   **Eustacia and Wildeve meet at the dance at East Egdon.**
They walk home together, but Wildeve leaves her when
they see Clym and Venn approaching. Venn has seen
Wildeve and indirectly lets him know this

Clym tries to comfort Eustacia in her bitter depression (a state which
causes her to contemplate death 'as the only door of relief', p. 318), but
he realises that she is now disillusioned with him. He still adores her
and, though he feels pangs of jealousy as she goes to the dance without
him, he encourages her to enjoy herself. She unexpectedly meets Wildeve
and they dance together. All the women, and especially Eustacia, are
intoxicated by the atmosphere and the moonlight. In this context,
Wildeve 'began to be a delight' (p. 323). They both resent the sense of
social constraint and feel that their now 'doubly irregular' relationship
could be resumed (p. 324). They walk home and part when they see Clym
and Venn approaching. Venn is sure he has seen Wildeve and, walking
rapidly to the Quiet Woman, he ascertains that Wildeve has been to East
Egdon to buy a horse. He tells Thomasin that he has seen her husband
returning with a horse, 'A beauty with a white face and a mane as black
as night' (pp. 327–8). When Thomasin asks Wildeve where the horse is,
he realises that Venn will again intervene in his relationship with
Eustacia.

> The dance and the moonlight stir the passions of the dancers and
> rational thought is overtaken by emotion; Eustacia seems to enter a
> dream-like state of rapture and is enchanted by the dance and by
> Wildeve. Recalling Eustacia's earlier prophetic dream of dancing
> with her hero, this scene demonstrates the marked difference in
> her perception of Clym now. The **imagery** of heat and cold reveals
> the great contrast Eustacia feels between her feelings as she dances
> with Wildeve and her life with Clym: 'outside, she had been steeped
> in arctic frigidity by comparison with the tropical sensations here'
> (p. 323). Her sexual desire is fired by the dance, the moonlight and
> the secrecy, and is a stunning experience in comparison with the
> lack of desire, love and hope in her relationship with Clym: 'She
> had entered the dance from the troubled hours of her late life as
> one might enter a brilliant chamber after a night walk in a wood'
> (p. 323).

Wildeve's desire, more than Eustacia's, thrives on the obstacles
which prevent their relationship: 'Obstacles were a ripening sun to
his love, and he was at this moment in a delirium of exquisite
misery' (p. 323). Like their previous relationship this new
development is equally based on selfish motives and a rebellion
against social restrictions and conventions; for Wildeve the fact that
both he and Eustacia are married makes his return to his former
lover 'compulsory' (p. 323). This episode signals the continuation of
the idea of 'fascination' (p. 322).

St Lazarus rattle in the Bible, Lazarus was the beggar in Jesus's parable
about the rich and the poor (Luke 16:19–31); he became the patron saint
of lepers, who carried a bell or a rattle to warn others away

CHAPTER 4   **Venn's 'silent system' deters Wildeve's clandestine
attempts to see Eustacia. Mrs Yeobright and Clym
both desire a reconciliation**

Aware that Wildeve is neglecting Thomasin, Venn feels compelled to
help. He employs what he calls his 'silent system' to try to deter Wildeve's
romantic feelings for Eustacia. Tying tufts of grass together, he causes
Wildeve to fall heavily; seeing Wildeve signal to Eustacia that he is
waiting outside the house, Venn knocks on the door then disappears
forcing Wildeve to leave; he then shoots at Wildeve. Wildeve realises the
seriousness of Venn's intent, but is determined to see Eustacia and will
call on her legitimately as a relative. Venn tells Mrs Yeobright of Clym's
impaired vision and also of his own attempts to hinder the relationship of
Wildeve and Eustacia. He encourages her to call on Clym and Eustacia
and this coincides with her desire for reconciliation. Simultaneously,
Clym also expresses his desire for reconciliation with his mother and
Eustacia reluctantly agrees to try to heal the rift between them and Mrs
Yeobright.

The reasons that Clym and his mother give for seeking
reconciliation are very similar, and Mrs Yeobright's phrase 'only
son' is echoed by Clym (pp. 334, 335). This emphasises the
strength and crucial importance to each of them that the mother-
child bond has, as is emphasised in the earlier narrative comment

that 'he was part of her ... their discourses were as if carried on
between the right and left hands of the same body' (p. 247). Despite
a separation, their bond remains close.

coup-de-Jarnac an underhand or unexpected blow; refers to the battle of
Jarnac (1569)
Strafford ... Virginia Farmer Lynch was Captain William Lynch (1742–1820)
responsible for unofficial justice meted out to looters during the American
Revolution; hence the term 'Lynch Law'

CHAPTER 5   **Mrs Yeobright makes a hard journey to Clym's house
in the fierce August heat. Seeing another man enter
the house after Clym, she approaches the door**

On the last day of August, Mrs Yeobright sets off for her son's
house in the fierce heat of the midday sun. Advised by a labourer to
follow the furze-cutter just ahead of her in order to find Clym's
house, she is shocked to realise that this 'parasite of the heath' is
her son and plans to save Clym and Eustacia from this degraded
'mode of life' (p. 339). Mrs Yeobright, feeling exhausted, agitated and
unwell, sits in the shade of some fir trees by the side of Clym's
house and deliberates how to approach this reconciliation without
enraging Eustacia. She sees a man enter the house and, thinking that
the presence of another may make her entrance easier, she approaches
the door.

> Once again Clym is identified as an insignificant part of the heath.
> His mother's view of him as a parasite on the heath and her plans
> to release Clym and Eustacia from this way of life reveal the
> similarities between Eustacia and Mrs Yeobright. The mounting
> heat is dangerous and the threat it represents is vividly conveyed:
> the sun is **personified** and seems to have 'branded the whole heath
> with his mark'; words associated with terrific heat, 'kiln' and
> 'incineration', suggest the stifling effects of the heat (p. 337). There
> is no relief in this landscape for this elderly woman; even the colours
> of the foliage and sky, which usually have a cooling and relaxing
> effect on the eye, contribute to the harsh glare – the sky is 'metallic
> violet' and the foliage resembles 'metallic mirrors' (pp. 338, 341).

The trees under which Mrs Yeobright sits symbolically mirror her own physical and emotional exhaustion, 'splintered, looped, and distorted by the fierce weather' (p. 340). Just as earlier the storm-beaten beeches predict Clym's emotional and physical suffering, so these trees add to the strong sense of foreboding which steadily increases throughout the chapter.

gait of Ahimaaz Ahimaaz brought the news to King David of the defeat of his enemy, Absalom (in 2 Samuel 17); the watchman recognised his distinctive way of running

the birthplace of Shakespeare ... Hougomont historic places of interest

CHAPTER 6   **No one opens the door to Mrs Yeobright and on her journey home her emotional exhaustion contributes to her dramatically deteriorating physical state. Johnny Nunsuch accompanies her some of the way, but most of the journey is made painfully slowly and alone**

Clym is asleep on the hearth when Wildeve arrives; Eustacia and Wildeve discuss Eustacia's marriage and their past relationship. Seeing that it is Mrs Yeobright at the door, Eustacia is agitated because of what her mother-in-law will think to find Wildeve there. They hear Clym stir and say 'mother' and assume he will answer the door. Wildeve leaves by the back door. Several minutes pass before Eustacia realises that Clym is still asleep, but when she opens the door Mrs Yeobright has gone. With a sense of utter dejection and shock Mrs Yeobright makes her painful way home. Johnny Nunsuch accompanies her for a while, but when Mrs Yeobright sits down to rest, Johnny goes on without her. The sun is now at its height and seems intent on consuming Mrs Yeobright, 'like some merciless incendiary, brand in hand' (p. 351), as she creeps along. Resting on a thyme patch she observes a colony of ants and a heron and thinks again of Clym.

Wildeve's elegant appearance contrasts dramatically with that of Clym asleep on the hearth. His sympathy for Eustacia's situation and admission that he married Thomasin as a reaction to Eustacia's behaviour reveals his continuing desire for her. She is dishonest with him, however, and suggests that she only began another relationship because he did, whereas we know that she had given Wildeve up before Clym returned.

It is an unlucky coincidence that Wildeve visits at the same time as Mrs Yeobright, but it seems to be Eustacia's guilt more than fate at this point which determines events. Her anxiety about her relationship with Wildeve again causes her to behave in a way which leads to Mrs Yeobright's distress, this time with more tragic consequences. Johnny's function is to make us (and later Clym) fully aware of Mrs Yeobright's utter exhaustion and bitter desolation. The fact that he is a child also builds a sense of tension because, although Johnny keenly observes Mrs Yeobright's state (making the reader fully aware of the acute danger of her situation), unlike an adult he is uncertain of how to help. In a state of collapse, Mrs Yeobright sees a colony of ants whose ancient ancestry and their 'never-ending' toil **symbolise** the insignificance of her life on the grand evolutionary scale of things, and also her rootedness to the heath which is indifferent to her plight (p. 351). The sight of a heron, 'dripping wet from some pool in the valleys' and free, makes her long either for similar refreshment, or for death and freedom from her crushed physical and emotional state (p. 351). Inevitably, her thoughts turn towards Clym and the meteor **image** encapsulates the intensity of her feelings for him.

marnels marbles
ooser a grotesque mask

CHAPTER 7   **Clym's dream about his mother needing help prompts him to visit her. He finds his mother, who has been stung by an adder, and the heath folk make a folk remedy**

Clym awakens from a prophetic dream in which his mother was calling for help; Eustacia does not tell him of his mother's visit and fails in her attempt to deter him from going to Blooms-End. His determination to go that day is strengthened by the fact that his mother must be lonely, since Thomasin's pregnancy would prevent her from visiting her aunt. That evening, as he pauses at the patch of shepherd's-thyme on his way to Blooms-End, he is shocked to find his mother exhausted and struggling to breathe. He carries her to within one mile of home and, leaving her to rest in a shed, runs to Fairway's cottage to fetch help. A boy is sent to fetch a doctor and to inform Thomasin of her aunt's illness. Revived by brandy, Mrs Yeobright indicates that she has been bitten by an adder. They prepare an old cure and Clym applies the adder fat to his mother's foot.

> The door between mother and son remains literally closed in this chapter (as the title of the book and Clym's dream suggests); however, the rift between Clym and his mother is **symbolically** healed in several ways. The connection between them is suggested by Clym's unconscious recognition of her knocking and by his dream; the time of Clym's dream, when his mother was lying collapsed in the thyme, also suggests a deep bond between them and it is as if her thoughts of him trigger it. His shocked recognition of the collapsed figure as being his mother echoes Mrs Yeobright's shocked recognition of her son in his furze-cutting clothes. This re-recognition of each other is significant symbolically because it demonstrates that their parent-child bond has survived the massive disruption of the rift between them. The momentary feeling of being transported back to his childhood bond with his mother and, returning to the present, the feeling that the 'chasm in their lives' is forgotten makes clear that the division is being healed (p. 356). This symbolic renewal of the bond between mother and son is important to the development of the **plot** and it explains Clym's response to Eustacia later. Although we can see that Mrs Yeobright's death was not entirely caused by Eustacia, our emotional involvement with this tragic episode and with Clym's deep regret initially bias us against Eustacia.

> A sense of tension is built up by the juxtaposition of the comic and the tragic in the shed as Clym and the heath folk try to cure Mrs Yeobright. The incongruous combination of Christian's ridiculous superstitious fears, Grandfer Cantle's comic boasting, and the increasing certainty of Mrs Yeobright's death seems to highlight the **absurdity** of the development of this **tragedy**.

Although as a modern man Clym doubts the folk cure Sam proposes, his desperation forces him to try anything.

Aeneas Aeneas carried Anchises, his father, out of Troy when the Greeks captured it

a dab at the hautboy an expert at the oboe

CHAPTER 8   **After hearing of Wildeve's fortune from her grandfather, Eustacia meets Wildeve on the heath. On their way to Blooms-End they pass the shed and overhear the tragic events unfolding inside. Eustacia returns home**

Feeling annoyed and agitated about the day's events and the probable consequences for her, Eustacia decides to go for a walk. As she is leaving the house, her grandfather calls with news of Wildeve's £11,000 inheritance and chastises Eustacia for not marrying him. Thinking of Wildeve's visit in this new light and of what his words and glances could have meant, she is surprised when he appears at her side. They walk towards Blooms-End and Wildeve tells her of his plans to travel and to eventually settle in Paris. As they pass the hut, Eustacia realises who is inside. By this point the doctor has arrived and Eustacia and Wildeve witness Mrs Yeobright's death from outside the hut. Johnny tells his mother what Mrs Yeobright had said about being 'a broken-hearted woman and cast off by her son', causing Clym much pain (p. 368). At first Eustacia wishes she had opened the door, but blames fate for the events; however, by the end of the chapter she acknowledges that she is to blame and that 'evil' is in store for her. Wildeve and Eustacia part and Eustacia looks back and sees everyone walking towards Blooms-End.

In this chapter we see Wildeve and Eustacia moving closer together. Their dreams of escape are the same, and even focus on the same destination, Paris. Paris is perceived in this novel as a showy and superficial place, a contrast in every way to Egdon, being in Wildeve's words, 'the central beauty-spot of the world' (p. 365). Their similar feelings about Mrs Yeobright also unite them, and their compromised position, especially given their past relationship, prevents both of them from offering help to their spouses. It seems apt that they should be literally outside the circle of family and friends who try to save Mrs Yeobright; they merely watch and overhear because they would rather selfishly protect themselves than offer comfort. However, any facile moral judgement of them based on the fact that their actions directly led Mrs Yeobright to struggle home and to her death (a judgement seemingly reinforced by their literal position outside the group so desperate to save Mrs Yeobright) is put into question by Clym's presence inside the group. Arguably Clym's delay in visiting his mother is as blameworthy as Eustacia's delay in opening the door, and Hardy refuses to allow simplistic moral judgements to be made.

There have been many echoes of Shakespeare's **tragedy** *King Lear* so far, especially in the last two chapters; this adds a solemn weight to the events and contributes to the sense of this tragedy being more profound than the 'players' on the heath would necessarily suggest (see Narrative Techniques).

sniffing courting

Hoffman, Mead ... Abbé Fontana Friedrich Hoffman (1660–1742) was a leading German doctor and medical theorist; Richard Mead (1673–1754) was a prominent English doctor; Felice Fontana (1730–1805) wrote a famous medical book

Book fifth: the discovery

CHAPTER 1   Three weeks have passed since Mrs Yeobright's funeral and Clym is ill with remorse and utter despair. Thomasin visits and Wildeve and Eustacia speak secretly

It has been three weeks since Mrs Yeobright's funeral and Clym, bitter with regret and despair, has been delirious for a week; he constantly chastises himself about failing to be reconciled with his mother. Thomasin visits and tries to comfort him. When Wildeve calls to collect Thomasin, Eustacia goes out and they speak of the secret which is making Eustacia 'wretched' (p. 377). Wildeve claims that Eustacia is not made for such sadness and they agree not to mention that Wildeve was in the house when Mrs Yeobright called. As Wildeve and Thomasin drive away, Wildeve sees Eustacia's pale face watching from the window.

> The repeated phrases and **imagery** in this chapter create a sense of the extent of Clym's' despair and his obsession with his guilt and regret. They also develop the **themes** of blindness and moral judgement and heighten the tension. Clym's sense of guilt, regret, grief and betrayal are repeatedly expressed in terms of his sense of having sinned against his mother. Biblical echoes about sin and forgiveness (beginning with Christian's reference to Eve's Original Sin when discussing his superstition about the adders, p. 359) become more pronounced. Echoing Christ's words on the cross, Clym asks Eustacia to forgive him, 'Forgive me for it Eustacia, for I scarcely know what I do', and Eustacia likens her guilty feelings to those of Christ's betrayer, Judas Iscariot (p. 374) and calls herself 'the sinner' (p. 377). Clym feels that his near-blindness was a punishment from God, but calls for more severe punishments for his sins. References to blindness are also repeated in this chapter and recall Mrs Yeobright's warning that Clym is blind in his judgement of Eustacia. The **metaphorical** sense of blindness here suggests that there will be an absence of joy and positive emotions for Clym, 'there is no light for me', as he takes 'the whole burden' of guilt upon himself (p. 373).

As Clym returns again and again to the fact that his mother did not visit him, Eustacia becomes increasingly distraught. The fourth repetition, 'My door has always been open to her – a welcome here has always awaited her. But that she never came to see', is intolerable to Eustacia and she tries to silence him (p. 376). The **dramatic irony** of these statements reaches its peak and the reader and Eustacia feel the danger of the mounting tension; Eustacia expresses her fear that when Clym discovers the truth he will kill her, 'for nothing else will be in proportion to his feelings now' (p. 378).

'Wherefore ... Misery' God allows Satan to tempt Job, and he curses the day that he was born (Job 3:20)

Judas Iscariot one of Christ's disciples who betrayed him and later hanged himself

> **Black Hole** refers to the Black Hole of Calcutta, a small cell in which one
> hundred and forty-six British people were imprisoned on a hot night in
> 1756; only twenty-three lived until the following morning

CHAPTER *2*   **Clym discovers the truth about his mother's visit**

After another month has passed, Clym is physically much recovered but
still silently brooding over the death of his mother. Christian brings news
of Thomasin's baby girl and also reveals Mrs Yeobright's intention of
visiting Clym on the day of her death. Hearing that Venn had spoken to
her, Clym instructs Christian to try to find Venn as soon as possible.
Clym goes to Blooms-End to sort out his mother's property and to make
the house ready for Eustacia to live in. Venn calls and is shocked to hear
of Mrs Yeobright's death. Venn assures Clym that his mother was
coming to see him on the day of her death and that she had completely
forgiven him. This contradicts Johnny's report and the following
morning Clym goes to visit the boy in the hope of solving the 'mystery'
(p. 384). Johnny reveals that he saw Mrs Yeobright's attempted visit and
also that Wildeve was in the house. This news confirms Susan Nunsuch's
conviction that Eustacia is a witch. In his fury Clym calls Eustacia a
murderess and sets out across the heath.

> Although Clym is in many ways a modern man, his reforming zeal
> is increasingly becoming dissipated in the face of the vast
> indifferent heath. At the beginning of this chapter he still intends
> to open a school, but he is nostalgic for the past and regrets that his
> mother's familiar and traditional family furniture will have to be
> replaced to accommodate Eustacia's 'modern ideas' (p. 382).
> Similarly, although he does not concur with Susan's superstitious
> views of Eustacia, the chill of the morning air as he approaches the
> Nunsuch's house is perceived as an omen, 'a thing of singular
> significance' (p. 385). Earlier he feels as if a 'fiend' had diverted him
> from his true duty to his mother (p. 373), and his anger at Eustacia
> several times causes him to speak of and to her in terms of
> witchcraft: she is 'a devil', threatens to 'bewitch' him again and
> brings 'a curse' upon him (pp. 390, 393, 394).

> His anger at the end of the chapter is a kind of blind rage, 'The
> pupils of his eyes, fixed steadfastly on blankness, were vaguely lit

with an icy shine' (p. 388). He is likened to Oedipus who, in Greek legend, blinded himself when he realised that he had committed incest with his mother. This suggests that the intensity of Clym's relationship with his mother and the fierce feelings he now has go beyond the laws of society; this state makes Eustacia's fear that he would kill her seem a possibility. However, his turmoil, like his mother's suffering, is insignificant in the face of the 'seamed and antique features' of the heath which seem to effortlessly absorb such human emotion (p. 388).

spudding digging
twanky annoyed, complaining
Ascension ... Fishes images of Jesus ascending to heaven after his resurrection (Luke 24:51), and the miraculous catch of fish (Luke 5)
black-hearts bilberries
Oedipus in Greek legend Oedipus unwittingly killed his father and married his mother; when he realised his crime he blinded himself in his anguish. The Greek playwright, Sophocles's drama *Oedipus Rex* (430BC) is based on this legend

CHAPTER 3   Clym accuses Eustacia of killing his mother and she refuses to admit that it was Wildeve in the house. Clym receives the news that Thomasin's baby is to be called Eustacia Clementine

Clym reveals that he knows the truth and angrily lays all the blame on Eustacia. Although shocked initially, Eustacia becomes callous and cruel in her response and refuses to admit that it was Wildeve whom Johnny had seen enter the house. Clym breaks into her desk and discovers an empty envelope addressed in Wildeve's handwriting, but, refusing to defend herself, Eustacia chastises him with the humiliation and unhappiness he has brought her. Finally, she breaks into sobs and tells him of her mistaken belief that he had woken up and let his mother in. In a trembling state Eustacia leaves. Shortly afterwards the servant informs him that Thomasin has called her daughter Eustacia Clementine, much to Clym's bitter disgust – he considers it 'a mockery' (p. 396). It does, however, continue to bind the four lovers for the future.

The heath renders Clym's rage and sense of loss insignificant; the thrush cracking a snail on the door-stone when he returns home symbolises this insignificance and predicts Clym's future of lonely survival. This feeling of the insignificance of human **tragedy** is countered, however, by the Shakespearean overtones of Clym's accusations. Phrases such as 'By my wretched soul you sting me, Eustacia! I can keep it up, and hotly too. Now then, madam, tell me his name' (p. 392) and 'Do you brave me? do you stand me out, mistress?' have a Shakespearean tone and, along with **allusions** to Shakespeare's *King Lear*, lend this scene a sense of profound and universalised human tragedy.

Our moral judgement of Eustacia is complicated further in this chapter; her callous reference to her sleeve and her wilful pride turn us against her, as does the suggestion that being Clym's wife is merely a role she now wishes to give up. However, their argument is framed by information which generates sympathy for her: the image of their faces in the mirror is a striking one and reflects her fear and sense of guilt; her suicidal tendencies convey her sense of despair, and her genuine distress (for once she is unaware of the effect her beauty is having) and her inability to tie her bonnet strings generate a feeling of pathos. These elements soften our response, as it would soften Clym's if he were not so determined to resist her. The fact that she mistakenly thought Clym had answered the door also generates sympathy for her.

adept in a certain trade   Clym accuses Eustacia of being a whore

CHAPTER 4   **Charley helps Eustacia to enter her grandfather's house. He realises her suicidal intentions and removes her grandfather's pistols**

After wandering uncertain of where to go, Eustacia returns to her grandfather's house, but he is out and the house locked. Charley is aghast to see her in such a state of despair; he breaks into the house and tries to make Eustacia comfortable by lighting fires and bringing her food and drink. The sight of her grandfather's loaded pistols in his room leads her to think of suicide. When she returns to get them, however,

Charley, who had guessed her intention, has removed them. He promises to keep her secret if she promises not to think of suicide anymore. Later her grandfather returns and orders her room to be made ready.

> Again we see a minor character playing an important function. There is a sense of appropriateness that Charley, who played a key role in the initial meeting of Eustacia and Clym, should now save her from a desperate action which is the result of the failure of that relationship. Thematically Charley is important as well: he epitomises the hero-worshipping kind of love which also characterised Eustacia's initial feelings for Clym. The barriers of social status which make it inevitable that Charley's love for Eustacia remains unrequited (since she is 'predestined to an orbit in which the whole of his own was but a point', p. 398), emphasise the inevitable failure of Eustacia's similarly impossible dreams which she built around her image of Clym as her hero. Eustacia's contemplation of suicide contributes to the sense of foreboding which is steadily building.

transportation the deportation of criminals to Australia

CHAPTER 5   **It is November 5 once more and Charley inadvertently signals for Wildeve to come. Eustacia meets him and Wildeve promises to help her escape to Paris**

After a week at her grandfather's house looking through his telescope, Eustacia sees her and Clym's belongings being moved to Blooms-End. She also sees Thomasin walking with her baby and the nurse. Charley assumes the role of guardian over Eustacia and on November 5 lights a fire to surprise and cheer her. Her mood, as she stares at the fire, is one of hopelessness. Hearing Wildeve signal his arrival, she is torn between an instinct to go inside and her desire to stay. At the second signal, her desire wins out. His pity for her (expressed several times since their dance together) now causes her to weep uncontrollably and he promises to help her however he can. Eustacia says she wants to go to Paris, but is uncertain about whether she wants Wildeve to accompany her. She will signal to him if she decides to go and Wildeve leaves.

CHAPTER 5 continued

A year has passed and the lives of some of the characters seem to mirror the cyclical passage of time: both Clym and Eustacia have come full circle in their return to their homes, and Wildeve and Eustacia are again planning their escape from the heath. However, there is an obvious change in Eustacia. She again uses her grandfather's telescope, but instead of this representing her ambition to escape the heath, it now signals her detachment from the lives of Clym and Thomasin as she observes them. This detachment mirrors the self-detachment she feels in the wake of the apparent cruelty of the gods and fate, for whom her suffering is merely 'sport' (p. 405). This sense of detachment from life **foreshadows** her ultimate detachment from life in death.

Wildeve feels renewed desire for Eustacia and tries to persuade her to allow him to escape from the heath with her; he twice reminds her of his wealth to try to tempt her. He assumes responsibility for her dilemma, which may be part of his attempt to win her love, but may also reflect his inflated idea of the role he played in her marriage to Clym. The reader is fully aware that Wildeve's actions had little, if any, effect on Eustacia's motivation to marry Clym, however; her cool attitude towards him now suggests her continued indifference to him as either 'a friend' or as 'a lover' (pp. 407, 408). Although she goes through the motions of making escape plans, she lacks the energy and hope that she had a year ago; she seems defeated by what she perceives as her inevitable destiny.

CHAPTER 6   **Clym visits Thomasin and explains his separation from Eustacia; Thomasin encourages Clym to write to persuade Eustacia to return to him. Wildeve returns home and Thomasin reveals that she knows the rumours about him and Eustacia**

At Blooms-End Clym has been repairing and preserving his mother's things for a week prior to the arrival of the furniture. Time has calmed the ferocity of Clym's anger and his feeling that he may have acted too rashly towards Eustacia accompanies his longing for her to return to him. On November 5 he visits Thomasin to try to ascertain Wildeve's reason for visiting his house on the day of his mother's death. Only Thomasin is at home (Wildeve is on his way to see Eustacia) and is shocked to hear of Eustacia's actions and Clym's new situation. Motivated by an unspoken suspicion that Wildeve is still interested in Eustacia, Thomasin encourages Clym to write to Eustacia to bring about a reconciliation. When he returns home, Clym writes a letter and determines to send it to Eustacia if she does not come to him by the following evening. When Wildeve returns later that evening, Thomasin challenges his night-ramblings alone and reveals that she followed him and knows that he has been to Mistover that evening. When Thomasin mentions the rumours she has heard about him and Eustacia in the past, Wildeve, aware that he is on dangerous ground, ends the discussion, thus enabling Thomasin to conceal Clym's visit.

> The repetitive patterning is strong in this part of the novel; added to the ominous comments and images, it builds a sense of anticipation of the fast-approaching **tragedy**. Thomasin's fear that Wildeve had 'fallen into the river' (p. 413) and Clym's delay in seeking reconciliation (a repetition of his delay in contacting his mother) leads us to expect tragic consequences. This delay does, as we see in the following chapter, contribute to Eustacia's decision to leave. A sense of the imminent failure of Eustacia and Wildeve's plans to escape is created by the fact that it was at this time of year, a year ago, that they similarly failed to escape (although for different reasons). Their sense of the heath being a 'gaol' (here reiterated by Thomasin) suggests that their attempts to escape will always be thwarted.

CHAPTER 7   **Eustacia attempts to escape the heath but fate, operating through coincidence, and the actions of others seem to conspire to prevent her**

Feeling that all hope of healing the rift with Clym is gone and with a sense of utter despair and alienation, not just from the heath but from the whole world, Eustacia resolves to leave Egdon. She is restless once she has packed and wanders on the heath, passing Susan Nunsuch's house; later she signals to Wildeve and he returns her signal. Fairway has forgotten to deliver Clym's letter earlier and Captain Vye leaves it on the mantelpiece until the morning. As he is about to go to sleep he notices that Eustacia's bedroom light is on and hears her go past his door, weeping. By the time he calls to her and realises what has happened, she has gone. She has not seen Clym's letter but, although Clym could have affected her decision earlier, at this point her plans are unalterable. With determination she sets out at midnight into the 'funereal' night, but on Rainbarrow realises that she has no money. Her pride will not allow her to ask Wildeve for money, nor allow him to accompany her; in utter despair she feels 'a captive still' (p. 420) and is 'broken' by the heath's malign power (p. 421). At the same time that Eustacia utters her final speech alone on the heath, Susan is melting Eustacia's effigy stuck with pins over the burning turf on her fire and speaking an incantation; the whole process was 'calculated to bring powerlessness, atrophy and annihilation on any human being against whom it was directed' (p. 422).

The chapter is organised into three sections, the events of which overlap to a certain extent, and each assumes a different point of view. This is a condensed version of the narrative technique employed throughout the novel, and is used to narrate the remaining chapters of this book. The overlapping events in this chapter highlight the factors which immediately contribute to Eustacia's failure to escape. These include her own romantic and impractical nature and her pride, coincidences, the failings and mistaken actions of others, and the general sense of resentment towards Eustacia, as well as the mystical powers (of witchcraft and the heath). The description of the night and the heath is excessively **symbolic**, mirroring Eustacia's excessive despair. The 'fleshy fungi' which resemble a dismembered animal strewn over the heath and the mention of the 'mouldered remains inside the tumulus' add a note of horror (p. 420); reference to biblical disasters magnifies the importance of the events on this night. Eustacia's final speech is like a **soliloquy** in a play, and reasserts her harsh experience at the hands of fate.

The **imagery** used to describe Eustacia's defeat finally draws together the repeated suggestions that Eustacia is an integral part of the heath. The heath seems to physically reclaim her and absorb her into itself. In utter defeat she crouches down 'as if she were drawn into the Barrow by a hand from beneath' (p. 420), and she seems to

melt into the heath as the rain and her tears form a continuous flow
into the earth, 'Between the drippings of the rain from her umbrella
to her mantle, from her mantle to the heather, from the heather to
the earth, very similar sounds could be heard coming from her lips;
and the tearfulness of the outer scene was repeated upon her face'
(p. 421). Susan's witchcraft intensifies this idea as the effigy of
Eustacia literally melts into the heath-turf being burnt by Susan.
The powers of the heath seem in accord with such activities, and
indeed there is a sense of demonic harmony between such
supernatural energy, the heath and its weather, and the 'chaos' of
Eustacia's mind (p. 420). This vivid and dramatic description
reinforces the complete inevitability of Eustacia's death on the
heath.

possett a drink used as a remedy for colds

the last plague of Egypt in the Bible to free the Israelites from Egypt, God
killed the first-born child of every Egyptian family (Exodus 12)

Sennacherib's host the destruction of one hundred and eighty-five thousand
Assyrian warriors in one night because of King Sennacherib's blasphemy (2
Kings 19)

Gethsemane the Garden of Gethsemane where Jesus passed his last night
before Judas betrayed him (Matthew 26:39)

CHAPTER 8   **Clym waits in vain for Eustacia to respond to his letter;
Thomasin tells him of her fears of Wildeve's elopement
with Eustacia. Captain Vye confirms Eustacia's
disappearance and Clym sets out to find them. Venn
helps to guide Thomasin to Wildeve's gig**

When Eustacia does not respond to his letter, Clym goes to sleep but is
awoken by Thomasin who arrives carrying her baby. She anxiously tells
him of her fears that Wildeve and Eustacia are planning to elope. Captain
Vye arrives with news of Eustacia's disappearance and thoughts of
suicide. Clym sets out in the continuing storm, shortly followed by
Thomasin. She loses her way but follows the light coming from Venn's
van. He is not there but returns a few minutes later having been looking
for a woman who had walked past his van weeping. Thomasin realises
that this must be Eustacia and, entrusting Venn to carry her baby,

instructs him to guide her towards home. They see the lights of Wildeve's gig lamps as they approach the inn and walk towards them.

A thorough sense of impending doom is created in this chapter as the wind and rain aggressively attack houses and people; the description of the wind against Clym's house, 'rasped and scraped', conveys a painful sensation (p. 424). Thomasin's suspicions have been aroused by the fact that Wildeve left the house with a large sum of money; there is much **dramatic irony** in view of Eustacia's desperate crisis on Rainbarrow which is prompted by her lack of money. However, as both Eustacia and Thomasin know, money is one way that Wildeve exerts control. He does not give Thomasin money and tries to claim her money as his own, and Eustacia knows that the debt she will owe to Wildeve if she takes his money would be an injury to her pride too much for her to bear. Money has already proved to be one source of disaster (the giving, gambling and receiving of money playing a key role in Mrs Yeobright's death), and the futility of Wildeve trying to use it to secure his hopes is stressed when the nurse pins his money up to dry after his death (p. 441).

The contrasts between Thomasin and Eustacia are maintained to the end; their different attitudes to the heath and to the violent weather again reveal the great differences between them. Although, like Eustacia, Thomasin experiences difficulties and discomfort in the stormy night, she has a rational and practical attitude: 'there were not, as to Eustacia, demons in the air, and malice in every bush and bough. The drops which lashed her face were not scorpions, but prosy rain; Egdon in the mass was no monster whatever, but impersonal open ground. Her fears of the place were rational, her dislikes of its worst moods reasonable' (p. 430).

The **imagery** of drowning which describes Thomasin's experience of the rain makes specific the disaster which is looming; she contemplates going out into the rainy night 'To plunge into that medium was to plunge into water slightly diluted with air', and the dripping foliage 'enclosed her like a pool' (p. 429). It may also suggest that she has some sympathy for what Eustacia experiences, although she would never allow herself to be so led by imagination and a sense of destiny.

Once again we see Venn trying to save Thomasin from public humiliation; she needs him to lead her to the right 'path' in a literal sense, although a more **metaphorical** meaning of moral path, or even path of life is suggested. Ultimately, he does lead her to what many consider the right path of happy matrimony.

Saint Sebastian the Roman emperor, Diocletian, tried to kill Sebastian with arrows for converting people to Christianity, he recovered but was then beaten to death

CHAPTER 9   **Wildeve and Eustacia drown in the weir, despite Venn's efforts to save them. Clym is saved but blames himself for Eustacia's death, as he blames himself for his mother's death**

The narrative slips back to Wildeve's preparations. He waits a quarter of a mile from the inn; however, instead of Eustacia, Wildeve's rival Clym appears. As Wildeve tries to conceal his identity, they hear the noise of a body falling into the stream. Clym arrives at the weir first and shines his lamp over the water; when Wildeve sees Eustacia's body floating he impulsively dives 'into the boiling cauldron' without taking off his heavy coat (p. 437). Clym, more cautious than Wildeve, balances his lamp before wading into the deeper part of the pool, but he too is drawn towards the powerful current at the centre where Wildeve is struggling. Venn arrives and sees a body floating. Quickly returning Thomasin's baby to her and instructing her to fetch help, Venn uses one of the upper hatches as a float. He rescues Clym who is unconscious; when he drags him out of the water, Wildeve is holding onto Clym's legs. Two other men arrive and help to find Eustacia. All three are taken back to the inn and a doctor sent for. Thomasin revives Clym with smelling salts, but the other two are dead. At four o'clock Charley, sent by Captain Vye, enquires about Eustacia. Venn tells him what has happened; Charley's request to see her is granted by Clym. Charley, Venn and Clym look at the bodies of Eustacia and Wildeve. Although he seems calm, Clym blames himself for the deaths of Eustacia and his mother.

At first Clym seems resigned to the disaster, but his comment that Eustacia is 'the second woman' he's killed that year reveals his disturbed state (p. 443). Clym blames himself, although he also has a sense that fate or the will of nature ultimately has the power to choose who to take: 'It would have been a charity to the living had the river overwhelmed me and borne her up' (p. 443). The blunt sentences he uses reveal his state of shock, though the rigid sentence structure also suggests that events are predetermined and, like this sentence structure, tightly controlled. Venn tries to comfort Clym and, as Thomasin did when comforting him about the death of his mother, he uses a rational, logical argument.

The predominant feeling in the final chapters of this book is that, regardless of human endeavour, fate will play out the events which have been anticipated throughout. Significantly, we cannot be sure whether Eustacia committed suicide or died by accident – in a sense it makes no difference, since ultimately her human will seems to have been subsumed by her sense of her destiny. Eustacia's repeated reference to a sense of being bound to the heath by fate is seemingly confirmed by her death in one of the streams which forms the boundary of the heath near to Shadwater Weir.

As Clym, Venn and Charley gaze on the body of Eustacia it seems **ironic** that in death she gains an almost angelic quality of light and seems at last to have found a suitable context for her dignity, stateliness and immense beauty. Wildeve too gains a 'luminous youthfulness' and our moral judgement of these two rebellious characters is softened by this final vision of them.

The novel was to end here, a year and a day after the story began with the **Aristotelian unities** of time and place preserved, as in Greek **tragedy**, thus elevating what may be seen as a tragedy of petty individual hopes and lives to something more profound and universal (see Narrative Techniques and Structure).

hartshorn smelling salts
Lazarus Jesus raised Lazarus, the brother of Mary and Martha, from the dead (John 11)

BOOK SIXTH: AFTERCOURSES

CHAPTER 1   **Eighteen months have passed, and Thomasin and her baby live with Clym at Blooms-End. Venn is now a dairy farmer and attends the Maypole celebrations at Blooms-End**

Rumours distort the scandalous story of Wildeve and Eustacia, though the tragedy accords them dignity. Thomasin returns home to Blooms-End in mourning for Wildeve and Clym becomes almost entirely withdrawn. On the day before Maypole-day, Venn comes to ask Thomasin's permission for the Maypole celebrations to take place outside her house. He has assumed his father's occupation of a dairy farmer and is no longer red. That evening Clym observes the Maypole-day preparations at Fairway's cottage and the following morning the air is perfumed by the Maypole flowers. Although Thomasin is eager to join in, Clym, fearful that Thomasin has romantic feelings for him, disappears. When he returns later that evening, Thomasin reveals that she did not go either. Venn, who is still lingering by the Maypole, declines her offer to come in because he wants to find a glove dropped by a young lady that day. Watching unseen from her window, Thomasin sees Venn find and kiss the glove and put it in his breast pocket.

> Clym's withdrawal from society is made explicit; he is now emotionally exhausted and full of bitter self-reproach. Alone on the heath, Clym has a sense of those who have peopled the heath in the past and that his existence is just part of an evolutionary cycle. This final book softens the message expressed throughout the novel that we live in an indifferent, if not hostile, universe, but Clym's sense of the insignificance of individual human lives in the grand scheme of things remains strong. The narratorial comment concerning the determined faith in a superior moral God, despite evidence to the contrary, suggests that religious belief is futile in the face of natural forces. Such ideas reflect the sceptical climate in which Hardy was writing and his own personal ideas (see Historical Background). The narrator also intrudes to record the customs of this part of the country; there is also a suggestion that the more pagan 'homage to nature' (p. 452) and celebration of life is a more apt system of belief.

Clym's fears that Thomasin has a romantic attachment to him, which he feels totally unable to reciprocate, blind him to what the reader can see is her real interest in Venn. Venn's reappearance bodes well; he is now a respectable farmer and Thomasin sees him as her social equal and, indeed, fully appreciates his improved appearance. In a sense, Venn is the native who most fully returns to the heath; he has always been in close physical contact with it, but now returns to participate in the social life and traditions as well. The season of early summer, with the natural world coming to life, and the pagan fertility celebration set the scene for new love to blossom. Hints that Venn is now using his artfulness to his own advantage to win Thomasin's love brings a sense of hope that Venn's devotion will finally be rewarded. Despite Clym's continued grief, this final book has an upbeat and hopeful atmosphere.

First Cause God

Babylon refers to the capture of the Jews by the Babylonians; they still remember Jerusalem and do not renounce the religion which has led to their captivity (Psalm 137)

CHAPTER 2   **Thomasin and Venn have a flirtatious meeting on the heath**

Thomasin is perplexed about whom Venn can be in love with, but Clym still fails to recognise Thomasin's feelings. When Rachel reveals that she borrowed and lost one of Thomasin's gloves at the Maypole celebrations and that Venn gave her money to replace them, Thomasin's thoughts are set spinning. Walking with baby Eustacia the following day, she meets Venn and they engage in flirtatious teasing and flattering; Venn's reference to his former courtship of her suggests his intention now.

Venn is now far more confident in his courtship of Thomasin and she herself rules out the obstacle of inequality that prevented their union in the past. There is a sense of the healing of old pains and losses, not only with the expectation that finally Venn and Thomasin will be united, but also with the choice of location for their meetings and the discussion of money. They meet in a spot where shepherd's-thyme grows, which reminds us of Mrs

Yeobright's death. Venn's teasing remarks about his single-minded concern with money recall, with some unease, the significance that money had in the unhappy marriage of Thomasin and Wildeve, and also in the development of the tragic events which culminated in the deaths of Mrs Yeobright, Wildeve and Eustacia. Here such associations and memories are transformed into something positive, as the spot and the teasing conversation draw Thomasin and Venn together with the sense of renewed love and hope for the future.

CHAPTER 3   **Thomasin agrees to marry Venn and Clym tells Humphrey his plans for becoming an itinerant preacher and keeping a night school**

Clym contemplates marrying Thomasin from a sense of duty to his dead mother's wishes, even though he knows that he is now emotionally and sexually dead, 'the mere corpse of a lover' (p. 460). Just as he is about to propose, Thomasin tells him of her plans to marry Venn. Clym is shocked and disapproves, largely because of his mother's opposition to Venn as a suitor to Thomasin owing to his inferior social status. In the following days Thomasin undermines this objection and Clym leaves it to Thomasin to decide, an indication of his increasing withdrawal from social interaction. A few days later Thomasin tells Clym that she is to be married on July 25.

> Clym's decision to propose to Thomasin is based on what his mother had hoped for, but is also influenced by the pragmatic approach to living which Humphrey expresses. Humphrey's argument that Clym and Thomasin should marry is based on the fact that ''Tis a pity to make two chimley-corners where there need be only one' (p. 464). Indeed, an element of pragmatism also seems to play a role in Thomasin's decision to marry Venn, as she repeats that she must marry Venn if she marries anyone (p. 462). Her decision is also clearly influenced by love and an appreciation of Venn's devotion; her second marriage is a contrast to her first in every way.
>
> The footnote, added in the 1912 Wessex Edition, suggests that Hardy felt that this happy ending was incongruous with the rest of

the **tragedy**. However, the ending is not entirely joyful because of the double and oppositional narrative and thematic strands that Thomas Hardy maintains in this last book. The sense of joy and continuity is tempered by regret and preoccupation with the dead, euphoria is balanced by pathos.

eleventh commandment there were ten commandments, but Jesus added another: to love thy neighbour

CHAPTER 4   **Venn and Thomasin marry, celebrate their marriage at Blooms-End and then leave for their new home. Clym takes up his vocation as an itinerant open-air preacher**

On the day of Venn and Thomasin's wedding the heath folk are again gathered, this time to make a mattress for the newlyweds. Their conversation reveals that they have changed little, although their mood is lighter and the tone somewhat mellower than when we first saw them. Christian seems to have matured a little since he can now criticise his father, and Grandfer Cantle, though still boastful and sprightly, seems to need assuring of his long life ahead. The newlyweds drive past as the heath men eat their lunch amidst the feathers. The mattress is later taken to Venn and Thomasin's house in Stickleford and the heath folk go to celebrate the wedding at Blooms-End. Clym does not join in, but writes his first sermon in his room. On the heath, Clym meets Charley, who is also still grieving for Eustacia; back at Blooms-End Clym gives Charley a lock of Eustacia's hair to remind him of her. As they return to the heath, Clym, unable to see well, asks Charley how the party is going. When Clym returns home, the party is over and Thomasin and Venn are about to leave. Now alone, Clym feels his mother's presence strongly and continues to reproach himself for his actions and loss. The following Sunday he preaches his first sermon on Rainbarrow; his text deals explicitly with a son's defiance of his mother's request. As time goes by he preaches in a variety of places to a variety of audiences and, although he is sometimes criticised, he is always kindly received.

In a scene which parallels the bonfire on the heath two and a half years previously, we see the heath folk engaged in a communal activity and discussing Thomasin's marital affairs. This time they are invited to celebrate the marriage and this bodes well for the future, since it suggests that Venn and Thomasin are in harmony with their community. The attitude of the fly driver emphasises the fact that Egdon is an isolated community and something of an oddity; the description of his gaze as 'supercilious' and his 'condescension' even to Thomasin and Venn invites criticism of such views and attitudes, however (p. 469). The reader is obviously not meant to judge this community negatively, although the inclusion of the view point of an outsider does help to bridge a gap between the world of Egdon and the world of the Victorian middle-class urban reader.

Charley's reporting of the celebrations to Clym as they stand outside the window emphasises Clym's poor eyesight. It also shows Clym's detachment and distance from such joyful celebrations of life and from social interaction: he refuses to join the celebrations and is physically unable to witness them. His decision to preach demonstrates that he is still an idealist and wants to serve others, and his first sermon signals that the rest of his life will be an expression of his self-reproach and deep remorse. The bitterness of this future is tempered, however, by the social impulses of his listeners and their human sympathy for his suffering.

Waxing a bed-tick coating the cover of a mattress with wax to stiffen it
racketing exciting
bruckle hit mistake
'Barley Mow' most well-known folk song, still sung in the twentieth century; a mow is a pile of straw
fly a covered carriage drawn by one horse
the skull at the banquet in Jacobean drama a skull was present at banquet scenes as a reminder of mortality
moral lectures or Sermons on the Mount Jesus's Sermon on the Mount is a very important aspect of Christian teaching (Matthew 5–7)
'And the king ... nay' Solomon told his mother, Bathsheba, that he would do whatever she asked, but he breaks his promise (1 Kings 2:19–20)

PART THREE

CRITICAL APPROACHES

CHARACTERISATION

Thomas Hardy introduces his characters in a very gradual way; hints and snippets of information build our anticipation and provoke our curiosity. Our initial uncertainty about who is who not only sharpens our attention, but also involves us in the world of the novel; we are like a visitor to Egdon Heath, slowly getting to know its inhabitants. The road on which we first see the characters adds to this sense of entering the world of Egdon. The way in which Venn, Captain Vye and Thomasin are introduced, as distant figures on a landscape which come into focus as we move closer to them, is a typical technique used by Hardy. Unlike many other Victorian novelists, such as George Eliot, Hardy does not provide a psychological dimension to his characters – we do not see the inner workings of their minds. Instead, their psychological states are externalised in the **symbols** and **metaphors** used and in their actions. Critics have suggested that unlike the characters created by George Eliot and Charles Dickens, Hardy's characters do not develop; rather we see the playing out of predetermined patterns of behaviour and responses.

This does not mean that Hardy's characters are in any way simplistic; the main characters in *The Return of the Native* are complex and have a duality or contradictory self-division which complicates their actions and responses. For instance, Clym is both a naive idealist and selfishly ambitious, he is a progressive thinker with a nostalgia for the past; Eustacia is a goddess and a foolishly romantic young woman. There is also a sense of conflict and balance between the characters; characters seem to contrast with each other, but these contrasts are often undermined and it is impossible to make clear moral distinctions. For instance, Clym and Eustacia seem to be contrasting characters in many ways, yet ultimately both selfishly seek to fulfil their own ambitions and try to use each other to do so. The moral distinction blurs further in the dilemma about who is to blame for Mrs Yeobright's death. It would seem to be a result of Eustacia's actions, but Clym's delay in seeking reconciliation implicates him equally.

Our response to the characters is also manipulated in a way which runs contrary to the morality typically endorsed in Victorian fiction where, as the Victorian dramatist Oscar Wilde quipped, 'The good ended happily, and the bad unhappily. That is what fiction means' (*The Importance of Being Earnest*, first published 1895, Methuen, 1966, p. 28). Eustacia's selfishness and illicit relationship with Wildeve should make us despise her and feel that she deserves to be punished, but instead we feel increasing sympathy for her. Although she and Wildeve are ultimately punished for their immoral behaviour, they are not condemned. Rather, in death Wildeve and Eustacia gain a luminosity, and Eustacia a 'dignity' and 'stateliness' which deliberately confuses the moral message.

The Return of the Native also seems to question the degree to which the characters are responsible for the **tragedy** which develops, and to what degree fate is in control and working through unlucky coincidence. Hardy categorised *The Return of the Native* as one of his 'novels of character and environment' and this suggests that innate characteristics and heredity are important factors. To a certain extent Novalis' dictum 'character is destiny' holds true, and we see how innate (and in Clym's case, inherited) characteristics, of stubbornness, passivity, pride, inflexibility and selfishness bring about the catastrophes that are in no way inevitable. In fact, it could be said that it is commonplace misfortunes and misunderstandings which affect the characters' lives. Throughout the novel, Eustacia blames fate for her destiny and for events, and her frequently repeated expectation of death on the heath seems to become a self-fulfilling prophesy. However, this could also be interpreted as her innate inability or wilful refusal to take responsibility for her life and mistakes, thus willing her fate. Her final crisis on Rainbarrow could be interpreted not as a fated catastrophe, but as a common oversight and a practical problem which could be solved. This seems to accord with Hardy's idea about how a **plot** or **tragedy** should develop, as he writes in a note in April 1878:

> A Plot, or Tragedy, should arise from the gradual closing in of a situation that comes of ordinary human passions, prejudices, and ambitions, by reason of the characters taking no trouble to ward off the disastrous events produced by the said passions, prejudices and ambitions.
>
> (*The Life of Thomas Hardy, 1840–1928*, Florence Hardy, Macmillan, 1962, p. 120)

Environment is also significant in the formation of character. The critic Ian Gregor relates the split in character, 'that bifocal view of character, so distinctive a feature in the novel', to the disparity between 'the vast impersonality of the heath and the claustrophobic intensity of the individual relationships of the Yeobrights' (*The Great Web: The Form of Hardy's Major Fiction*, 1974, p. 108). The different attitudes to the heath are also an indication of character: Eustacia's perception of it as a hellish prison suggests her neurotic tendencies, whereas Thomasin's attitude to it as 'a ridiculous old place' where she can live happily suggests her practical and rational nature (p. 462). The social and spiritual factors of this community can also be seen to contribute to the development of character; although this not always positive, as in Christian Cantle's case.

However, there is a strong sense of some mysterious forces in operation, and the chains of events which lead to the tragedies seem to be a result of a synchronicity of human failings and fate. Character and circumstances coincide and chance seems to dictate characters' actions and determine their responses.

CLYM (CLEMENT) YEOBRIGHT

Clym is a modern man and an idealist. From the first responses to this novel his idealism has been both criticised and applauded: 'a moon-struck dreamer, who seems singularly out of place among the eminently practical population of Egdon' (in R.G. Cox, ed., *Thomas Hardy: The Critical Heritage*, 1970, p. 54), 'a humanitarian' with a 'large appreciation of human duty' (in Cox, p. 70), and by the end of the novel, 'a more noble, more pathetic figure' than is found anywhere else in English fiction (in Cox, p. 89). He is the first of Hardy's failed idealists and seems to express Hardy's ambiguous attitude to the application of the socialistic and evolutionary ideas of the time to rural life (see Historical Background). He is wrong in his ideal of human desire for learning and his pursuit of this mistaken belief leads to his failure; the fact that his ideas are ahead of his time is also a determining factor in this failure. Critics have seen Clym as a partially autobiographical figure, despite Hardy's description of him as 'the nicest of all my heroes, and not a bit like me' (see Thomas Hardy – Life and Works). His motivation for return encapsulates the contradictory nature of his character: he longs to return home to the familiar, unchanging heath for which he has such nostalgic affection, yet he wants to change the organic social structures which exist there with his progressive scheme of education. He has admirable qualities, but his inflexibility and single-minded ambition invites criticism, and indeed contributes to the tragic events.

Clym gives up his prosperous and successful career as a diamond merchant in order to bring progress to Egdon Heath, to 'raise the class at the expense of individuals rather than individuals at the expense of the class' (p. 230). His philanthropic goals become modified, apparently under the influence of his mother and Eustacia, and he plans to open a private school for farmers' sons in Budmouth. However, this change also seems to reflect Clym's own underlying personal ambition, which drives him to single-mindedly pursue his goals at the expense of his relationships with his mother and with Eustacia, and at the expense of his health. His literal blindness is an externalised expression of his lack of perception: he cannot see that the ideals he seeks to put into practice are totally inappropriate to the needs of the heath folk, and that they are in conflict with the needs and ambitions of his wife and his mother. His return makes no sense to them and is a regression in their eyes. Although Clym is identified with the heath physically and emotionally, he is its 'product', he is also a product of his experience in Paris. The intellectual ideas he brings back to the heath make him a perpetual outsider to this community which is determined by its relation to the life forces of nature and the seasons, not by thought, which drains vitality.

His return to make his mark as a reformer and as a man 'who loved his kind' seems also bound up with a sense of needing to prove himself as a man. In his discussions with the heath men at the haircutting and in his first argument with his mother, he rejects his business in Paris as 'effeminate' (pp. 229, 233). His attraction to Eustacia is influenced by his perception of her as a vulnerable victim, allowing him to assume the manly role; when he first visits Eustacia, she has been attacked by Susan Nunsuch and also burns herself on the well rope. This brings out his tender feelings for her, and despite his natural asceticism, he is fascinated by the luxury even her wound represents: her needle puncture is 'like a ruby on Parian marble' (p. 244). Eustacia's repeatedly expressed fears that his mother will influence him against her also seem to play on his fear of emasculation and impotence, and twice force him into action (pp. 256, 266). In contrast, later, his passivity and procrastination in relation to his mother and Eustacia (he delays reconciliation with them) directly contribute to the tragedy which unfolds.

Clym is also the tragic hero of this drama, his **tragic flaw** being his blind idealism and single-minded ambition. He is also a kind of Christ figure, willing to be the first to be sacrificed in order to fulfil his mission to establish a new system for human development and fulfilment not based on worldly wealth. His survival suggests a rising from the dead, and finally he preaches his 'Sermons on the Mount' as Jesus did (p. 473).

EUSTACIA VYE

Many critics agree that Hardy's female characters are more engaging and plausible than his male characters. Certainly Eustacia is one of the most enigmatic of his characters. She is both 'Queen of the Night', a 'murderess' and a victim of fate; she is a divided character, experiencing a 'warring' within herself (p. 115). She is mythic, magnificent and full of pagan mystery and, simultaneously, a romantic young woman overwhelmed by the scope of her own fantasies. She is a contradictory mixture of languor and vigour, having a 'drowsy latency of manner which discovered so much force behind it whenever the trigger was pressed' (p. 204). Early critics likened her to Flaubert's Madam Bovary and remarked on her 'shallow heart' and 'uncultivated mind' (in Cox, p. 69), calling her 'a wayward and impulsive woman, essentially commonplace in her feelings and wishes' (in Cox, p. 54), and a 'coldly passionate heroine' seemingly unaware that 'such a thing as responsibility exists' (in Cox, p. 58). These and other comments do justice to some aspects of her character (her selfishness, sharp temper, manipulation, jealousy, pride, capriciousness), but they remind us also of the reasons for some of these negative aspects. She is given scant 'moral training' (p. 204) from her irresponsible grandfather, and although his lack of attention gives her the freedom to wander the heath, it also gives rise to excessive boredom and painful loneliness, described evocatively as 'the eating loneliness of her days' (p. 121). The tragic status that she achieves at the end of the novel and the shifts in sympathy towards her as she moves seemingly irrevocably towards her fate are not explained on this realistic, matter-of-fact level. Her mythic status surpasses her realistic identity, just as her fantasies and desires surpass what is humanly possible; this is a dilemma of which she is, however, well aware, as she says to Clym 'Nothing can ensure the continuance of love' (p. 255).

Her relationship with the heath is at the heart of her internal contradiction. She seems to be more of its 'product' than Clym and knows its paths intimately. She is thoroughly identified with the heath and has 'imbibed' its darkness; her unconventional beauty and behaviour mirror the heath's sublimity, and her association with night and social disruption parallels the darkening effect of the heath and its apparent disruption of diurnal and seasonal orders (as the November-like storm in summer demonstrates). Ostensibly, she longs to escape this prison in order to begin to really live, but she refuses three offers of escape (one from Venn, and two from Wildeve); she also seems easily defeated in the only real bid for freedom that she does make. This reinforces the fact that, at a **metaphorical** and fatalistic level, she is at one with the heath and, regardless of her will, she cannot leave. The final images of her in the storm suggest that she has been reabsorbed into the heath. Her conflict with it can be read as an externalised expression of her own inner conflict and self-denial.

As an outsider Eustacia is suspect, and her behaviour and isolation cause her to be labelled a witch. Her contemptuous attitude to the heath folk contributes to their negative perception of her. She was originally conceived as a witch in the manuscript version of the novel, and references to her supernatural and 'bewitching' powers recur throughout. Both Wildeve and Clym are fascinated with her (the archaic sense of 'fascinate' means to be under a spell), but neither can satisfy her intense yearnings for something more than her lot. Like George Eliot's dark and passionate heroine Maggie Tulliver in *The Mill on the Floss*, Eustacia is thwarted in her desires and ultimately killed by water.

The dichotomy of the dark and fair heroine, common in Victorian fiction and iconography and employed by Eliot and Hardy, suggests that Eustacia and Maggie's failure to attain their goals is partly a consequence of their clash with perceived ideas of what a woman should be. Privileging the fair heroine **symbolically** meant endorsing the ideal of Victorian femininity (angelic, pure and passive), and punishing the dark heroine was a warning against unfeminine, defiant and dangerous behaviour. Although ultimately Eustacia is seemingly punished by her death, this is not a simple endorsement of the dominant cultural values. As Rosmarie Morgan argues, in exploring Eustacia's 'smouldering rebelliousness' Hardy exposes 'the anger and frustration suffered by the intelligent mind and energetic body restricted to an unvarying, unchallenging, isolated existence' (*Women and Sexuality in the Novels of Thomas Hardy*, Routledge, 1988, p. 59). She is contrasted throughout with Thomasin, the fair, dutiful, practical woman, who is prepared to make the best of the life that is offered to her.

MRS YEOBRIGHT

Mrs Yeobright endorses conventional values and aspirations; she has a strong sense of personal, family and class pride and upholds social distinctions. She is a strong and controlling character, as is seen in her influence over Thomasin and her attempts to change Clym's decisions. Although she fails to prevent Thomasin and Wildeve's engagement, once Thomasin has been jilted she sees it as imperative for the sake of Thomasin's reputation that she marries Wildeve. Clym later criticises his mother's negligence in not finding out more about Wildeve's character, and insists that Thomasin's reputation would not have been ruined; what is implicitly suggested is that Mrs Yeobright is acting selfishly to protect her own respectability. Her opposition to Venn as Thomasin's suitor is similarly a sign of her social pride and her inflexibility, as is her rejection of Clym's ambitions. His refusal to accept that success can only mean social advancement and material gains contradicts her conventional views of success and is deemed 'wrong' because of this. She refuses to compromise, although this brings her much pain.

Obviously, there are great differences between Mrs Yeobright and Eustacia (especially given Eustacia's immoral behaviour and extreme unconventionality). However, she is similar to Eustacia in many ways; they are both jealous, irrational, wilful, self-centred, uncompromising, ambitious for success via Clym, and proud. Clym several times draws comparisons between them. She is also like Clym in her stubbornness; this similarity between them is a crucial factor in the development of the **tragedy**. All three are in their own ways rebels against the traditional ways of life on the heath – Clym wants to reform it, Eustacia wants to escape it, and Mrs Yeobright wants vicarious success through her son in Paris, not through his return to within its boundaries.

Although her narrow-minded inflexibility and pride invites criticism of her, our response to her is softened by mention of her more endearing qualities. She has an angry temper and is unpredictable, but also has a 'gentle mood' (p. 91). Narratorial comment also modifies our response. For example, when Mrs Yeobright's behaviour seems to be at its most unacceptable (as an irrational, possessive, jealous or even incestuous mother) in one of her many arguments with Clym over Eustacia, the narrator intervenes with a comment which generalises and universalises her response, thus making it more understandable: 'Hardly a maternal heart within the four seas could, in such circumstances, have helped being irritated at that ill-timed betrayal of feeling for a new woman' (p. 251). Similarly, our sense of pity for her is aroused when she collapses in the intense heat on the heath; her intention in visiting Clym had been good and her bitterness at what she perceives as his rejection of her gesture of reconciliation is understandable. Even in her state of utter exhaustion she thinks of Clym and is to the last his devoted mother.

She is also realistic and right in respect of Clym's new occupation for which he has no special qualifications; Budmouth is 'overrun with schoolmasters … What possible chance is there for such as you?' She is also right in her criticism of his choice of Eustacia as his wife and helpmeet. As Clym realises, 'his mother was so undoubtedly right' having a 'singular insight into life' (p. 248).

THOMASIN

Thomasin is everything that Eustacia is not: she is quiet, obedient, patient, sweet, gentle, practical, showing filial respect and a rational response to the heath; she is the enduring wife of Wildeve, and finally a survivor living a conventional life as part of the local community. Whereas Eustacia is associated with night (her hair absorbs or obscures light, it 'closed over her forehead like nightfall extinguishing the western glow', p. 118), Thomasin is repeatedly associated with light (her face is 'luminous', p. 89 and her hair reflects the sunlight like 'a mirror', p. 215). Whereas Eustacia is passionately romantic, Thomasin is aware of romance as a youthful dream, as she says to Wildeve: 'Here I am asking you to marry me; when by rights you ought to be on your knees imploring me, your cruel mistress, not to refuse you, and saying it would break your heart if I did. I used to think it would be pretty and sweet like that; but how different!' (p. 95). Whereas Eustacia is associated with mythic figures and goddesses, Thomasin is associated with the **pastoral** and birds (p. 271).

She is in many ways the Victorian ideal of femininity and is passive rather than active; although she can be spirited, as in her vehement resolve to marry Wildeve, and can also be commanding, as in her relationship with Venn. Her marriage to Wildeve places her in a submissive role which she does not overtly challenge, except for her hints that she knows of his infidelity. Hardy seems to be offering an indictment of marriage and women's lack of power within it in his negative portrayal of how Wildeve exercises his power over Thomasin by his (legal) control over his and her money (see Historical Background).

DAMON WILDEVE

Like Eustacia, Wildeve is an outsider, who considers himself to be sophisticated and superior to the heath folk. Like her, he is selfish, discontented, ambitious, impulsive, romantic and unconventional in his passions; in fact, only illicit relationships seem to stir his desires. He comes to the heath under the shadow of a failed career as an engineer, and longs to escape it. When he does finally have the money to go, he plans to settle in Paris, the place of Eustacia's dreams as well.

An early critic called him 'a man of the world and a gay and fascinating Lothario' (in Cox, p. 52), and he is explicitly depicted as a physically attractive philanderer, though his 'lady-killing career' has something of a 'pantomimic expression', thus mocking the charming sophistication he thinks he has (p. 93). Mrs Yeobright disapproves of him and her suspicion and distrust remain justified. She demands that he 'make no false representations' to her, but this is what he repeatedly does over his marriage to Thomasin (p. 93). He is an opportunist and has a vindictive side to his personality. He finally marries Thomasin in order to spite Eustacia, with whose games he has become impatient; likewise, he initially tries to win the guineas from Christian as revenge for Mrs Yeobright's lack of trust. He is deceitful, as is illustrated by his thoughts of answering Eustacia's signal fire even while he is keeping up the pretence of being married when the heath folk come to celebrate his wedding.

By way of reassuring herself before their marriage, Thomasin asserts that he is not cruel: 'You who cannot bear the sight of pain in even an insect, or any disagreeable sound, or unpleasant smell even, will not long cause pain to me and mine' (p. 96). However, once married to Thomasin he treats her unkindly, if not cruelly, and in denying her money keeps her under his control. His poking the glowworms and signalling to Eustacia by sending a moth into her candle flame are small but **symbolic** denials of Thomasin's claim. They are cruel acts which he selfishly hopes will help to satisfy his desires (of winning back the money, or of calling Eustacia to him), regardless of the consequences for others.

DIGGORY VENN

Venn is not so much of a divided character, although his strange supernatural associations as a reddleman belie his highly conventional desires and ambitions. He has been subject to two distinct interpretations, however. He is either 'a benign agent of order within the community', trying to make things work out for what he sees as the good, or a voyeuristic, 'moral watchdog who, mirroring the Victorian puritanical conscience, fulfils the role of censor' (as Rosmarie Morgan suggests in *Women and Sexuality in the Novels of Thomas Hardy*, Routledge, 1988, p. 66).

'Diggory' is a dialectal term for the devil, and in Hardy's original conception he was to have been an agent of the devil. He comes close to this more dangerous, if not demonic, function when he shoots at Wildeve to deter his nocturnal visits to Eustacia. Morgan argues that the 'malevolent', hidden side of his character is slowly revealed and she criticises his perpetual 'meddling' and his repeated failure 'to get his facts right' (Morgan, pp. 68, 69). Although his interventions do unintentionally speed up the tragic events, his altruism, self-renunciation, devotion and disinterested actions (which the selfish Eustacia and Wildeve cannot comprehend), honesty, patience and humble acceptance of his lot (as far as a relationship with Thomasin goes) express Christian values. His final reward, not in heaven but in Book 6, expresses a pattern of relationships common in Hardy's fiction between

'The Poor Man and the Lady'. Venn is shrewd, independent and enduring.

In a sense it is Venn, not Clym, who is the true native who has returned. As both a reddleman and as a dairy farmer following in his father's footsteps, Venn continues in the traditions of this heath community. As a reddleman his supernatural associations similarly associate him with the customs of this area, as well as link him explicitly to the land (reddle is a dye derived from clay) which his itinerant trade allows him to know intimately. Venn returns to his native place four times, finally settling in a relationship which ensures 'The Inevitable Movement Onward' (as the first chapter of Book 6 is titled) and a continuation of the social life and customs of the heath. Venn and Clym also seem to mirror each other; as Venn gives up his itinerant life, Clym takes it on.

THE HEATH FOLK

The heath folk add a comic dimension to the novel, especially Christian's excessive and foolish superstition and Grandfer Cantle's sprightly boastfulness. Early critics likened them to the comic relief of Shakespearean rustics and both praised the dialogue as witty and criticised its oversophistication. Although some critics have detected a note of condescension in Hardy's depiction of the natives of the heath, they do have vitally important functions in the novel, not least the preservation of the local dialect, and the folklore customs and the festivities of this area. They are the primary participants in the ritualised celebrations which Hardy sought to record and preserve, celebrations which have ancient origins, although subsequent eras have shifted the associations. The bonfire on November 5, the Christmas mumming, the Maypole dance and the 'gypsying' all have pagan origins and mark the changing of the seasons. Their superstitions and witchcraft (attacks such as that on Eustacia took place in Dorset as late as the 1880s), folk remedies, fatalistic outlook on life and celebrations of marriage are part of Hardy's documentation of 'a vanishing life'.

This is not their only purpose, however. They are crucial to the development of the **tragedy** and have the specific narrative function of acting as a **chorus**, commenting and speculating on the lives of the main characters in a way which is often prophetic. Their comments are often perceptive and have profound significance. Christian in particular plays a crucial function in the development of the tragedy when he gambles with Clym's and Thomasin's money. His comments about chance and the powers of the dice, 'powerful rulers of us all', reflect his naivety, but also highlight the fact that the lives of many of the main characters seem to be tragically fated. Christian has a parallel role with Venn who, although intending to do the right thing, unwittingly makes matters worse.

RECURRING THEMES

The interrelated **themes** of conflict, ambition and love recur throughout *The Return of the Native*. The ambitions of the characters often bring them into conflict with other characters, with the established traditions and values of their society, and with their environment. Their ambitions also highlight their internal conflicts and expose their self-delusion. There are many expressions of love in this novel (romantic, sexual, filial, maternal, selfish and altruistic) and love relationships often act as a focus for the development and expression of conflict.

    The parent-child conflict between Clym and Mrs Yeobright, caused by Clym's ambitions and love for Eustacia, is both a clash of values and ideas and a psychological power struggle. Clym's values clash with his mother's – he is fiercely progressive and Mrs Yeobright is fiercely conventional. At a psychological level he strives to win his independence from this powerful maternal force. This clash between them also seems to be an externalised representation of Clym's inner conflict. Their love for each other remains deep and the description of the intensity of their relationship suggests that they are one body, 'he was part of her ... their discourses were as if carried on between the right and the left hands of the same body' (p. 247). This **image** suggests that the conflict between them is one person's internal conflict. Clym's internal dilemma is suggested further by the fact he does not doubt his ability to persuade his mother to accept his views, but is anxious about whether or not he would be right to do so. This suggests his uncertainty about his plans for change when he is still so drawn to the past.

Love relationships also become a focus for Eustacia's conflict with the social and physical environment of the heath, and also expose her internal conflicts. Her secret and illicit relationships with Wildeve are a rebellion against conventional social values, and her marriage to Clym is her best chance of rebelling against the heath by escaping it. The inability of either of her lovers to satisfy her needs and desires highlights the inner conflict that Eustacia feels, a conflict which is externalised in her relationship with the heath. It is her prison, but it also accords her the dignity which, in the society of Paris or even Budmouth, would be denied her. There she would not be the unique, commanding and mysterious figure that she is in this heath community, but would, rather, be an average young woman of slender means.

Only the characters who are not in conflict with the heath and its traditions, nor with themselves live happily ever after. Venn, Thomasin and the heath folk are the only ones left unscathed at the end.

The theme of return is also strong in this novel and has a predominantly negative meaning. In the case of Clym, his return home with the purpose of bringing reform to the heath results in failure; his ideas clash with those of the community, and his impetus for change seems to dissipate in the face of the unchanging heath. The heath folk and his mother consider this return to be a regression, and return is similarly a regression in terms of evolutionary theory. 'Return' is also used by Clym in the sense of the profit made from an investment; at the peak of his bitter remorse about his mother's death he considers that his mother has a poor 'return' for her personal investment in him (p. 373). Wildeve and Eustacia both seek to return to a more sophisticated life and are similarly doomed to failure. Venn repeatedly returns to the heath and although he tries to make things work out for the good, neither his intentional nor accidental interventions can apparently alter fate. It is only in his final return to the heath and to the dairy farmer he always should have been that a return has a positive outcome.

NARRATOR

Like many other Victorian novelists Hardy uses the technique of the **omniscient narrator** in *The Return of the Native*; this is an impersonal narrator who not only tells the story, but intrudes into the narrative with asides, digressions, philosophical reflections, **ironic** observations, pictorial vignettes, **allusions** to art and literature and factual information. The omniscient narrator assumes a superior understanding of the characters and the capacity to speak the truth unproblematically; this is called the **hierarchy of discourses** in **classic realist texts** and has also been criticised for its didacticism. According to Janice Carlisle in *The Sense of an Audience: Dickens, Thackeray, and George Eliot at Mid-Century* (The Harvester Press, 1982), the characteristic use of a narrator as a mediating presence between the reader, the text and the author was one means by which Victorian novelists fulfilled what they saw as their moral responsibility as writers.

However, the delivery of a clear moral message is not Hardy's aim, and although the narrator does guide our responses to a large extent, there is a degree of ambiguity about how we are to judge the characters. For instance, after the short period of romantic passion between Clym and Eustacia is over and Clym has decided to work as a furze-cutter, we are told that Eustacia has a 'forlorn look about her beautiful eyes which, whether she deserved it or not, would have excited pity in the breast of any who had known her during the full flush of her love for Clym' (p. 317). The narrator is guiding us to feel some sympathy for Eustacia, but is also leaving it to us to decide whether or not she 'deserved' it. The narrator at times seems to have quite a cynical attitude to the characters, as in his comment about Clym that 'if he were making a tragical figure in the world, so much the better for a narrative' (p. 226).

REALISM

Hardy adopts the nineteenth-century literary convention of **realism** although, as many critics have suggested, he seems to find this convention limiting and breaks with it. According to Michael Wheeler, Victorian writers used the convention of realism 'to engage directly and consistently with the complexities of human experience in the real world'

(*English Fiction of the Victorian Period 1830–1890*, Longman, 1985, p. 7). By presenting a fictional world which resembles the real world, realism stresses the sincerity of representation and hence hopes to engage the reader's sympathies. Hardy also aimed to create a record of a vanishing rural life and to this end his realism merges with regionalism. He documents the customs, traditions, class structures, and dialect of this area; he creates a realistic setting which is based on a recognisably real place, and provides a map so that correspondences between the fictional and the real world are obvious. Hardy was not alone in basing his fiction in a real place, and the leading Victorian novelist Anthony Trollope earlier set his *Barchester Towers* (1857) in a recognisably real setting.

However, his earliest critics noted that Hardy failed to sustain the impression of verisimilitude and they saw his use of coincidence, improbability, fatalism, sensationalism and **melodrama** as a major flaws in his writing. Later critics, such as Terry Eagleton and Peter Widdowson (see Critical History) argue that his breaks with realism are a deliberate strategy.

The heath is one aspect where we can see this break with realism: it is simultaneously realistically created using geographical, topographical and natural historical detail; but it is also an imaginary, **metaphorical, symbolic** and mystical landscape. In real terms it is a tract of land which can easily be crossed in a day, but is overwhelmingly vast in its non-realistic sense. It also functions as a kind of microcosm and as a stage set. That this break with realism is deliberate can be inferred from the distinction Hardy draws between realism and art:

> Art is a disproportioning – (i.e. distorting, throwing out of proportion) – of realities, to show more clearly the features that matter in those realities, which, if merely copied or reported inventorially, might possibly be observed, but would more probably be overlooked. Hence 'realism' is not Art.
>
> (*The Life of Thomas Hardy, 1840–1928*, Florence Hardy, Macmillan, 1962, p. 229)

The convention of realism is mimetic and aims to create a mirror reflection of life; thus the literary techniques used are disguised. Hardy's writing, however, highlights the techniques he uses, such as coincidence and suspense.

COINCIDENCE AND SUSPENSE

The insistent and unlucky coincidence which seems to drive the narrative in *The Return of the Native* does reveal the important reality that Hardy wants to convey – that the universe and fate are indifferent, if not hostile, to humanity. Narrative **foreshadowing** creates the sense of the inevitability of fate, and we are drawn into the narrative by the suspense that Hardy builds up. This sense of suspense is created at the beginning of the novel by the fact that the first book is comprised of a series of beginnings, with connections and narrative development only occurring gradually. This means that the unfolding of the narrative strands is deferred, and the reader is kept waiting. The story of Thomasin's failure to marry is begun as she is carried in Venn's van and the reader may expect that Captain Vye's curiosity would lead to the unfolding of her story. Instead this narrative development is deferred, with suspense being built by hints and implications, until Chapter 5. The story of the figure on Rainbarrow similarly does not begin to be fully unfolded until Chapter 6. The gambling scene is another example of Hardy's effective use of suspense (Book 3, Chapter 8).

CINEMATIC TECHNIQUES

Hardy's narrative techniques, like those of many other Victorian realist writers, seem to anticipate filmic techniques. The critic David Lodge has referred to him as a 'cinematic novelist' (see David Lodge, *Working with Structuralism: Essays and Reviews on Nineteenth and Twentieth Century Literature*, Routledge, 1981). Hardy's frequent use of obvious shifts in points of view, which enable us to see events through the eyes of different characters as they spy on or observe others, resembles cinematic techniques. The shifts in narrative focus from the landscape to a character's face or some natural detail readily compare with the cinematic techniques of long shot, panoramic view, close-up, zoom and panning. For example, in the second chapter the narrative focus shifts from the perspective of an unspecified observer who sees the unnamed Captain Vye, to Captain Vye's gaze along the road on which he sees a speck which as he comes closer is revealed to be the unnamed Venn; we then follow Venn's gaze as it pans over the landscape, moving up to the barrow and zooming in to focus on the figure there.

USE OF ALLUSION

The Return of the Native is rich in reference and **allusion**. Thomas Hardy has been accused by some critics of being pretentious, but the allusions to other literary texts, plays, the Bible, artistic techniques and artists, science, myth, and historic figures add many levels of meaning. One significant reference is to Shakespeare's *King Lear*. Hardy refers to the legendary King Lear in his Author's Preface to the novel and there are echoes of the themes and actions of Shakespeare's play throughout, especially in Mrs Yeobright's experience of rejection by her son. *King Lear* explores the themes of the parent-child bond, pride, arrogance, misunderstanding, justice, blindness and madness and there are echoes of these throughout Hardy's novel. The effect is to heighten and universalise the sense of tragedy. The legend of Oedipus and reference to Sophocles' tragic play about this legendary figure similarly intensifies the sense of tragedy.

STRUCTURE

Hardy's break with **realism** can also be seen in the integration of dramatic aspects into his fiction. *The Return of the Native* was intended to consist of five books, mirroring the five acts of a Greek **tragedy**, with a prologue and epilogue, and a **chorus** to comment on the action. It was to maintain the **Aristotelian unities** of time, place and action, with the story being confined to a year and a day, events being confined to the heath (described in places like a stage set), and the action following a cause-and-effect sequence. There are many references to acting and playing a role, and in places the dialogue of the characters resembles the speeches found in Elizabethan and Jacobean drama. Clym's accusation of Eustacia is reminiscent of Shakespearean tragedy, and Eustacia's final speech very much resembles a **soliloquy**.

Repeated patterns add a sense of unity and harmony. The seasonal cycle and the traditional celebrations provide repeated social events between which the private drama develops. The similarity of scenarios and actions draws attention to the structure of the narrative development: Venn leading Thomasin home after her failure to marry Wildeve at the beginning is paralleled in the later scene of him supporting her and leading a cart carrying her dead husband, his mistress and Clym in Book 5. This scenario is finally echoed at the end when Venn and Thomasin depart together in the dogcart to their new life. There are also cyclical patterns in the novel, for instance Clym replaces Eustacia as the figure on the barrow, although her brooding dissatisfaction and longing for a future away from the heath contrasts starkly with Clym's bitter resolve to do penance for his sins and to cherish the past. Coincidence is obviously a key factor in the **plot** development and often provides turning points in the narrative structure.

The Return of the Native is framed in such a way as to draw the Victorian middle-class urban readers into the world of the novel, and then gradually return them to their reality with a warning not to disparage Egdon Heath and its community. Comments in the first chapter resemble the kinds of observations made by Victorian travel writers and so put the reader at ease with this harsh landscape: 'spots like Iceland' in the future will be as familiar and appreciated as 'the vineyards and myrtle-gardens of South Europe' (p. 55). The description of the fly driver's attitude to the anachronistic life on the heath as 'supercilious' suggests that the reader is not to judge this community negatively, as he does. The inclusion of the view point of an outsider does help, however, to bridge a gap between the world of Egdon and the world of the reader as the reader prepares to leave this fictional world.

STYLE, IMAGERY AND SYMBOL

Many critics have argued that what Hardy calls his 'living style' is merely careless and clumsy, and point to the excessive and sensational aspects of his writing as flaws. Others have attempted to appreciate the range of styles he employs. In her essay 'The Novels of Thomas Hardy', Virginia Woolf comments on Hardy's style: 'No style in literature, save Scott's, is so difficult to analyse; it is on the surface of it so bad, yet it achieves its aim unmistakably' (in R.P. Draper, ed., *Thomas Hardy: The Tragic Novels*, 1991, p. 79). Hardy's linguistic range is evident in the language the narrator uses which is sometimes formal, complex, intellectual and often adopts an **ironic** tone, yet is also exaggerated, inflated and highly wrought in some of the descriptive passages. Hardy's description is very visual; it is self-consciously pictorial in places, as in the frozen image of Clym (Book 2, Chapter 6), as well as ostentatious, as in his picture of Eustacia (Book 1, Chapter 7). This range of styles is deliberately employed in order to generate a specific response in the reader, as well as to develop the **themes** of the novel. For instance, his use of irony tends to distance the reader from the characters, but also intensifies the sense of the inevitable workings of fate. His use of distanced description, as in the aerial views of Clym as a 'brown spot' on the heath (p. 312) and Eustacia and Wildeve's faces 'like two pearls on a table of ebony' (p. 325), emphasises the theme of the insignificance of humanity on an indifferent landscape or in a hostile universe.

His powers of description engage us imaginatively, intellectually and emotionally; his style is evocative, vivid and highly poetic. *The Return of the Native* has been called 'Hardy's greatest nature poem' (Robert Langbaum, *Thomas Hardy in Our Time*, 1995, p. 64). Hardy's description has a number of functions; most obviously it is used to create certain atmospheres and moods, but also crucially it often **foreshadows** difficulties and disasters, some of which characters may be half aware, but which they do not want to admit. For example, the eclipsed moon **symbolises** the very different dreams that Eustacia and Clym have about their marriage and has ominous implications for their marriage.

Hardy's **imagery** is often sensuous and symbolic; Eustacia's relationship with the heath is often conveyed in such a way. For example, her first movement is **metaphorically** 'the glide of a water-drop down a bud' as she descends from the barrow (p. 63). Later her death and absorption back into the body of the heath is more explicitly suggested, as she crouches down she feels 'as if she were drawn into the Barrow by a hand from beneath' (p. 420). Hardy uses images to do with seeing and perception (eyes, mirrors, reflections), which emphasise the sense of being watched – an important feature of the plot – and which externalise psychological states; Clym's blindness is an obvious example of this. The weather imagery has a prophetic function, and also externally expresses the highly charged emotions which largely remain unspoken. Bird imagery is used to convey a sense of character (Thomasin is likened to birds, for instance), and also symbolises emotional states: Mrs Yeobright's release of the trapped sparrow, her only living companion, on the day of Clym and Eustacia's wedding symbolises her resigned acceptance to let go of her only son (p. 275). Contrasting imagery of light and darkness pervades the novel, emphasising the dualities which run throughout: good and evil, perception and blindness, reason and irrationality, harmony or discord with Nature, love and hate.

The powerful and striking images help to convey a sense of the strangeness of ordinary life, as well as the sense that mysterious forces are at work. The imagery associated with the heath is highly prophetic, and the heath itself symbolises the forces of nature against which humans struggle, as well as a universe indifferent to human tragedy.

TIME

References to time in the *Return of the Native* have a structural and thematic significance. From the first line of the novel it is clear that seasonal time and festivities will be important. These seasonal celebrations organise the cyclical time scale in the novel, although with their reference to ancient and pagan rituals of the past, they also suggest the coexistence of the past and present. At the bonfire '[i]t was as if these men and boys had suddenly dived into past ages, and fetched therefrom an hour and deed which had before been familiar with this spot' (p. 67). It is as if the past and present merge in such rituals, a blurring of time which other references in the text also suggest (Clym's awareness of the past inhabitants of the heath, for instance).

The comic discussion of the heath folk about which measurement of time is the true one points to the futility of human attempts to exert control over time (p. 186). We are told that 'On Egdon there was no absolute hour of the day', and the heath itself seems to control diurnal and seasonal time, darkening the daylight, and prolonging the winter. The heath is described in terms of its ancient, unchanging and timeless qualities, and such description raises philosophical questions about human existence and evolution. The more specific time references in Book 5 also work to increase the tension by reminding us of the rising heat as the summer months pass. The date of Mrs Yeobright's death is one of the few specific date references in the whole novel and this demonstrates the importance of this event.

PART FOUR

TEXTUAL ANALYSIS

TEXT 1 (PAGES 67–8)

Moreover to light a fire is the instinctive and resistant act of man when, at the winter ingress, the curfew is sounded throughout Nature. It indicates a spontaneous, Promethean rebelliousness against the fiat that this recurrent season shall bring foul times, cold darkness, misery and death. Black chaos comes, and the fettered gods of the earth say, Let there be light.

The brilliant lights and sooty shades which struggled upon the skin and clothes of the persons standing round caused their lineaments and general contours to be drawn with Dureresque vigour and dash. Yet the permanent moral expression of each face it was impossible to discover, for as the nimble flames towered, nodded, and swooped through the surrounding air, the blots of shade and flakes of light upon the countenances of the group changed shape and position endlessly. All was unstable; quivering as leaves, evanescent as lightening. Shadowy eye-sockets, deep as those of a death's head, suddenly turned into pits of lustre: a lantern-jaw cavernous, then it was shining; wrinkles were emphasized to ravines, or obliterated entirely by a changed ray. Nostrils were dark wells; sinews in old necks were gilt mouldings; things with no particular polish on them were glazed; bright objects, such as the tip of a furze-hook one of the men carried, were as glass; eyeballs glowed like little lanterns. Those whom Nature had depicted as merely quaint became grotesque, the grotesque became preternatural; for all was in extremity.

Hence it may be that the face of an old man, who had like others been called to the heights by the rising flames, was not really the mere nose and chin that it appeared to be, but an appreciable quantity of human countenance. He stood complacently sunning himself in the heat. With a speaker, or stake, he tossed the outlying scraps of fuel into the conflagration, looking at the midst of the pile, occasionally lifting his eyes to measure the height of the flame, or to follow the great sparks which rose with and sailed away into darkness. The beaming sight, and the penetrating warmth, seemed to breed in him a cumulative cheerfulness, which soon amounted to delight. With his stick in his hand he began to jig a private minuet; a bunch of copper seals shining and swinging like a pendulum from under his waistcoat: he also began to sing, in the voice of a bee up a flue –

'The King´ call'd down´ his no-bles all´,
By one´, by two´, by three´;
Earl Mar´-shal, I'll´ go shrive´ the queen´,
And thou´ shalt wend´ with me´.

'A boon´, a boon´, quoth Earl´ Mar-shal´,
And fell´ on his bend´-ded knee´,
That what´-so-e'er´ the queen´ shall say´,
No harm´ there-of´ may be´.'

The attention has shifted from the timeless and impassive heath and the few individuals on it, to the communal human activity on the top of Rainbarrow. It is a passage which illustrates the shifts in tone and perspective found frequently in *The Return of the Native*, and it explores the human relation to this landscape.

Apparently detached from the rest of the heath in this 'radiant upper storey of the world' (p. 66), the heath folk, like their ancestors, express their defiance of the darkness of winter and the oppressive atmosphere which dominates the heath. The first paragraph is elevated in its tone, shifting from mythical reference to biblical **allusion**. The instinct to defy Nature's winter 'curfew' with light is likened to the daring act of the legendary Greek hero, Prometheus, who stole fire from the gods in order to give it to man and was cruelly punished as a result. This figure symbolises the resistance to oppression, but also unmerited suffering, anticipating the rebellion and suffering of the 'Promethean heroes' of this novel, Eustacia and Clym. The language of the final sentence resembles that of a sermon, and the order, 'Let there be light', echoes God's words in the first verses of Genesis with which he divided night from day. Hardy uses many biblical allusions and his Victorian readers, more familiar with the Bible than the majority of modern readers, would have readily inferred their meaning. Here biblical allusion seems to highlight the coexistence of pagan and Christian beliefs which runs throughout the novel. On the whole, however, pagan belief seems to predominate, and the way that Christianity is subsumed by the more ancient religion is demonstrated here by the fact that biblical language is used to convey an essentially pagan impulse.

From this focus on humanity's active defiance of Nature, God and the human lot, attention shifts in the second paragraph to the effects of the fire on the appearance of the revellers. It is the fire's 'lights and sooty shades' which are now active as they struggle on the skin and clothes of the people by the fire. The humans are passive and it is the fire which, in its creation of light and shadow, can alter the appearance entirely; it has the power of concealing or revealing. In the flickering firelight, '[a]ll was unstable' and appearance alters radically with the shifting light and shadow. This also suggests a more profound instability in the distinction between the humans, the fire and the landscape. The description of the 'nimble flames' which 'towered, nodded, and swooped' creates the sense of an animate being through use of **personification**, 'nodded', 'swooped' and the adjective 'nimble', which is usually associated with human actions. The use of **alliteration** also seems to suggest a sense of unity between the fire and the human figures in its light; the repetition of 's' suggests some connection between the 'sooty shades' which 'struggled' and the 'skin' of those 'standing' round.

Similarly, although the heath folk feel detached from the 'vast abyss' of the heath (p. 66) and even at war with it as they defy Nature's dictates, the description of the effects of the shifting firelight suggests a connection between the landscape and these individuals. Their faces are described in terms of the landscape – 'pits', 'ravines', 'cavernous' – and alliteration of the 'r' sound in 'ravines', 'ray' and 'wrinkles' again suggests a sense of unity. Thus, this passage maintains the blurred distinction between the animate and inanimate, the passive and active, which has characterised this landscape from the opening description of the heath as a vast tract of impassive land and an animate being. The relation of the inhabitants to the heath is now seen to have a similar duality; they are seemingly both in rebellion with it and held in thrall to its mysterious powers and forces. This duality is a constant thread throughout the novel.

The firelight is transformative, it defamiliarises and exaggerates human features and everyday tools in a deceptive way, and puts everything into 'extremity'. This anticipates some of our feeling about Eustacia, a character whose fiery passions, Promethean rebellion, extreme desires and suspected associations with witchcraft, is firmly identified with fire. Her meetings with Wildeve by her bonfires involve deception, either of each other or of other characters. She signals to Wildeve with fire in the hope of achieving her impossible ambitions and passions. Here, too, on Rainbarrow the fire is a signal to call members of the community, and to make connections with the surrounding parishes; Eustacia's fire, however, emphasises her distance and isolation from such communal experience.

The fire on Rainbarrow has acted as a signal for Grandfer Cantle. The third paragraph now shifts from the generalised description of anonymous figures in an ambiguous relation to the fire and the heath, to the specific as individual characters gradually emerge. In the previous paragraph the human figures are seemingly turned into objects in the light of the fire: **metaphors** and **similes** liken them not only to the landscape, but to other inanimate objects: 'sinews in old necks were gilt mouldings', and 'eyeballs glowed like little lanterns'. In this paragraph the focus shifts to an individual's response to the fire; he is 'complacently sunning himself in the heat'. The tension between whether the fire or the humans are in control now seems resolved in a co-operative relationship between Grandfer Cantle and the fire: he feeds, monitors and observes it and he gains pleasure from its warmth. There is a sense of harmony and balance as the warmth from without produces a warmth from within, and the fire fills him with 'cheerfulness, which soon amounted to delight'. He then expresses this delight in his dancing and song, and an old man, as his voice like 'a bee up a flue' and later comments suggest, is filled with renewed vitality and goodwill. This description seems to be making a general point about the heath folk's survival of the heath's darkest season through communal good will and good cheer, as well as introducing us to this character's eccentricity. This eccentricity is suggested by the incongruity of his beginning 'to jig a private minuet', and his unexpected dress, 'a bunch of copper seals shining and swinging like a pendulum from under his waistcoat'.

This method of introducing characters first as anonymous objects which gradually emerge as individuals is a typical device used by Hardy, as we have seen in his introduction of the 'speck' which is revealed to be Venn, in the previous chapter. This extract is typical of the novel in other ways as well: it explores the duality of the landscape and human existence on it. The description is very visual and emphasis on eyes and perception becomes increasingly important as the novel goes on, as does the use of images of light and darkness on this virtually colourless landscape. It raises the issue of making moral judgements and just as it is 'impossible to discover' 'the permanent moral expression of each face', so it will be

TEXT 1 continued

impossible to make a definite moral assessment of characters and their actions. Finally, the centrality of fire not only hints at the rebellion to come, but suggests that survival in such a location is only possible by communal effort. The song which Grandfer Cantle sings at the end of this passage, and the onus on pagan ritual which the Bonfire celebration as a whole suggests, is significant to Thomas Hardy's aim of recording the vanishing rural life and customs of his native Dorsetshire.

TEXT 2   (PAGES 161–3)

Eustacia was indoors in the dining-room, which was really more like a kitchen, having a stone floor and a gaping chimney-corner. The air was still, and while she lingered a moment here alone sounds of voices in conversation came to her ears directly down the chimney. She entered the recess, and, listening, looked up the old irregular shaft, with its cavernous hollows, where the smoke blundered about on its way to the square bit of sky at the top, from which the daylight struck down with a pallid glare upon the tatters of soot draping the flue as seaweed drapes a rocky fissure.

She remembered: the furze-stack not far from the chimney, and the voices were those of the workers.

Her grandfather joined in the conversation. 'That lad ought never to have left home. His father's occupation would have suited him best, and the boy should have followed on. I don't believe in these new moves in families. My father was a sailor, so was I, and so should my son have been if I had had one.'

'The place he's been living at is Paris,' said Humphrey, 'and they tell me 'tis where the king's head was cut off years ago. My poor mother used to tell me about that business. "Hummy," she used to say, "I was a young maid then, and as I was at home ironing mother's caps one afternoon the parson came in and said, 'They've cut the king's head off, Jane; and what 'twill be next God knows.'"'

'A good many of us knew as well as He before long,' said the captain, chuckling. 'I lived seven years under water on account of it in my boyhood – in that damned surgery of the *Triumph*, seeing men brought down to the cockpit with their legs and arms blown to Jericho … And so the young man has settled in Paris. Manager to a diamond merchant, or some such thing, is he not?'

'Yes, sir, that's it. 'Tis a blazing great business that he belongs to, so I've heard his mother say – like a king's palace, as far as diments go.'

'I can well mind when he left home,' said Sam.

''Tis a good thing for the feller,' said Humphrey. 'A sight of times better to be selling diments than nobbling about here.'

'It must cost a good few shillings to deal at such a place.'

'A good few indeed, my man,' replied the captain. 'Yes, you may make away with a deal of money and be neither drunkard nor glutton.'

'They say, too, that Clym Yeobright is become a real perusing man, with the strangest notions about things. There, that's because he went to school early, such as the school was.'

'Strange notions, has he?' said the old man. 'Ah, there's too much of that sending to school in these days! It only does harm. Every gatepost and barn's door you come to is sure to have some bad word or other chalked upon it by the young rascals: a woman can hardly pass for shame some times. If they'd never been taught how to write they wouldn't have been able to scribble such villainy. Their father's couldn't do it, and the country was all the better for it.'

'Now, I should think, cap'n, that Miss Eustacia had about as much in her head that comes from books as anybody about here?'

'Perhaps if Miss Eustacia, too, had less romantic nonsense in her head it would be better for her,' said the captain shortly; after which he walked away.

'I say, Sam,' observed Humphrey when the old man was gone, 'she and Clym Yeobright would make a very pretty pigeon-pair – hey? If they wouldn't I'll be dazed! Both of one mind about niceties for certain, and learned in print, and always thinking about high doctrine – there couldn't be a better couple if they were made o' purpose. Clym's family is as good as hers. His father was a farmer, that's true; but his mother was a sort of lady, as we know. Nothing would please me better than to see them two man and wife.'

In this passage Eustacia, who has heard of Clym's imminent return from her grandfather, overhears a conversation between her grandfather, Humphrey and Sam which provides more information. It also confirms the importance of such a return to this small and isolated community.

Coincidence and eavesdropping have already become significant in the novel (Johnny has overheard Wildeve and Eustacia and related their discussion to Venn, a coincidence which alerts Venn to the illicit relationship between them) and will continue to be crucial to the development of the **plot**. However, coincidence and eavesdropping never result in a positive outcome, despite good intentions.

At this point in the novel, Eustacia has acknowledged that she no longer wants Wildeve and that the time is ripe for a better man to take his place. Everything she hears from this conversation convinces her that Clym is the ideal man: he is young, has settled in Paris and is manager to a diamond merchant. Humphrey's description of Clym's occupation as 'a blazing great business … like a king's palace, as far as diments go' suggests the life of exotic wealth, luxury and excitement that Eustacia craves. The reference to royalty would confirm Clym as the ideal match for the 'Queen of the Night' and 'blazing' seems apt as far as Eustacia's fiery personality and passionate ambitions go. Their discussion continues to create an appealing impression; he is probably quite rich and is educated. Humphrey's comment that 'to be selling diments' is better than 'nobbling about here', can only reaffirm Eustacia's desire to escape. Their comments about his being a 'perusing man, with the strangest notions' anticipates their response when he returns and tries to put such notions into practice, especially given their apparent indifference to the school, and the Captain's hostility to education.

It is the conversation that Humphrey and Sam have when Captain Vye has gone, however, which really fires Eustacia's imagination. They draw parallels between Eustacia and Clym's social positions and match-make them as 'a very pretty pigeon-pair', expressing the pleasure it would give to see them married. As at several other points in the novel, the heath folk play an important function in their influence on the lives of the main characters (an obvious example is the impact of Christian's gambling). As we see repeatedly, their words are often prophetic, and here Sam and Humphrey's conversation seems to affect Eustacia's behaviour and anticipates future events. It also adds to the rising expectation associated with Clym's return.

Their gossipy conversation has the important function of drawing together two of the main narrative strands which are driving the **plot** on – Clym's return and Eustacia's longing to escape. The union of these two characters would clearly be contradictory, and a warning of their incompatibility is implicit in Humphrey and Sam's mistaken assessment of Eustacia as 'always thinking about high doctrine'. Clym and Eustacia are well-matched in terms of being educated, but it is Eustacia's total disinterest in 'high doctrine' that Humphrey, Sam and, later, Clym mistake. This adds a note of foreboding to the idea of Clym and Eustacia's apparently ideal union. Significantly, Eustacia ignores this inaccurate description of herself, focusing rather on what she wants to hear; likewise, she later ignores the reality of her relationship with Clym in her persistence with her fantasy of going to Paris.

This overheard conversation sends Eustacia off into her dream world for the rest of the day. The fact that Wildeve is now obliterated from her romantic fantasies is evident when Humphrey and Sam's discussion of Eustacia's former rival for Wildeve, Thomasin, has no effect on Eustacia.

This passage raises the issue of social status which is important, especially to Eustacia and Mrs Yeobright, and which has such an impact on the unions which develop. Venn, who is so clearly an ideal partner for Thomasin, is refused because of his inferior status, and Eustacia similarly considers Wildeve to be below her. Although the heath folk see Clym and Eustacia's social status as equal, Mrs Yeobright does not and this forms one element of her disapproval of Eustacia later. Social distinctions are implied by the fact that the heath folk speak using a Dorsetshire dialect which distinguishes them in terms of class from Captain Vye. However, his superior social status does not automatically accord him respect, and Humphrey and Sam mostly either ignore or contradict his narrow-minded views.

Although this passage anticipates the development of a relationship between Eustacia and Clym, it also sounds several ominous notes. In addition to the one mentioned above, the guillotining of the king during the French Revolution undermines the glamour which Humphrey associates with Clym's business in likening it to a king's palace. Further, Eustacia's position in the recess of the chimney looking up at the square of sky at the top suggests her hope of escape and seems an apt place for her fiery passions and fantasies to be stirred. However, the **imagery** of the light at the end of this tunnel, as it were, is not positive: 'daylight struck down with a pallid glare'. The **simile** of 'soot draping the flue as seaweed

TEXT 2 continued

drapes a rocky fissure' suggests that Eustacia is **metaphorically** in an underwater world, longing for light and air which are only glimpsed here. Such an image is reminiscent of Eustacia's desperation to escape the heath, her gasping for life. It also anticipates her failure to escape this suffocating environment and her death by water as she makes her final bid to achieve her ambitions.

TEXT 3   (PAGES 322–3)

Through the length of five-and-twenty couples they threaded their giddy way, and a new vitality entered her form. The pale ray of evening lent a fascination to the experience. There is a certain degree and tone of light which tends to disturb the equilibrium of the senses, and to promote dangerously the tenderer moods; added to movement, it drives the emotions to rankness, the reason becoming sleepy and unperceiving in inverse proportion; and this light fell now upon these two from the disc of the moon. All the dancing girls felt the symptoms, but Eustacia most of all. The grass under their feet became trodden away, and the hard beaten surface of the sod, when viewed aslant towards the moonlight, shone like a polished table. The air became quite still; the flag above the waggon which held the musicians clung to the pole, and the players appeared only in outline against the sky; except when the circular mouths of the trombone, ophicleide, and French horn gleamed out like huge eyes from the shade of their figures. The pretty dresses of the maids lost their subtler day colours and showed more or less of a misty white. Eustacia floated round and round on Wildeve's arm, her face rapt and statuesque; her soul had passed away from and forgotten her features, which were left empty and quiescent, as they always are when feeling goes beyond their register.

How near she was to Wildeve! it was terrible to think of. She could feel his breathing, and he, of course, could feel hers. How badly she had treated him! yet, here they were treading one measure. The enchantment of the dance surprised her. A clear line of difference divided like a tangible fence her experience within this maze of motion from her experience without it. Her beginning to dance had been like a change of atmosphere; outside, she had been steeped in arctic frigidity by comparison with the tropical sensations here. She had entered the dance from the troubled hours of her late life as one might enter a brilliant chamber after a night walk in a wood. Wildeve by himself would have been merely an agitation; Wildeve added to the dance, and the moonlight, and the secrecy, began to be a delight.

Whether his personality supplied the greater part of this sweetly compounded feeling, or whether the dance and the scene weighed the more therein, was a nice point upon which Eustacia herself was entirely in a cloud.

People began to say 'Who are they?' but no invidious inquiries were made. Had Eustacia mingled with the other girls in their ordinary daily walks the case would have been different: here she was not inconvenienced by excessive inspection, for all were wrought to their brightest grace by the occasion. Like the planet Mercury surrounded by the lustre of sunset, her permanent brilliancy passed without much notice in the temporary glory of the situation.

As for Wildeve, his feelings are easy to guess. Obstacles were a ripening sun to his love, and he was at this moment in a delirium of exquisite misery. To clasp as his for five minutes what was another man's through all the rest of the year was a kind of thing he of all men could appreciate.

Eustacia, increasingly depressed by Clym's persistence in his occupation as a furze-cutter and disillusioned with her marriage to him, has decided to go to the 'gypsying' dance alone. Meeting Wildeve there unexpectedly, she agrees to dance with him and although at first she has reservations, once she begins to dance and her pulse is racing she no longer thinks about what she is doing. The passage demonstrates clearly her changed feelings for Clym and emphasises her passionate nature, hinting also at a sexual relationship between Eustacia and Wildeve as they renew their bond. The frenzied dancing recalls the defiant dancing of the heath folk at the bonfire, and a similar sense of rebellion and the unleashing of anger and pleasure is created in this scene. The coincidence of their meeting, as with all other coincidences in this novel, does not bode well, however.

Dancing in the moonlight with Wildeve, Eustacia is intoxicated, revitalised and restored to her passionate self. The word 'giddy' suggests the dizzy sensation of the whirling energetic dance, which reminds us of Eustacia's youth and creates a sense of release from her dull life with Clym. The word is highlighted by the unusual **syntax** which positions it towards the end of the clause. The archaic meaning of giddy was 'mad' and in this atmosphere the senses are unbalanced and 'dangerously ... tenderer moods' are promoted. The use of this term and the description of effect of the dance recalls Eustacia's passionate desire '[t]o be loved to madness' (p. 121). As emotions are stirred, the irrational behaviour increases; the **alliteration** of 'r' in the 'rankness' of emotions which increases as 'reason' decreases highlights the contrast between the two: such emotion is not rational, and the word 'rank' implies both the vigorous increase of emotion, and the sense of its immorality.

As she dances, Eustacia is in a trance-like state of rapture, and the whole scene recalls her earlier dream about the 'ecstatic' dance with her lover-hero, with the heath forming a dim background to 'the brilliancy' of the action (pp. 173–4). In her prophetic dream her lover-knight 'fell into fragments', and here we see how her illusion of Clym as that hero is now similarly shattered, and how Wildeve could, temporarily at least, replace him. In her dream she and the knight dived into one of the pools on the heath, anticipating the death of Eustacia and Wildeve. Here the description of Eustacia's rapture is also reminiscent of their death: she 'floats' with Wildeve and her face is expressionless because 'her soul had passed away from and forgotten her features'. Such **symbolic** patterning and repetition are key features of this text.

The **imagery** of heat associated with the dance and Wildeve is sexually suggestive and contrasts starkly with the imagery of Eustacia's sexually and emotionally frozen life with Clym: 'outside, she had been steeped in arctic frigidity by comparison with the tropical sensations here'. Her sexual desire is fired by the dance, by 'treading one measure' with Wildeve, and by the sensation of feeling each other's breathing. The moonlight and the secrecy add to the 'enchantment', and the whole experience is stunning in comparison with the lack of desire, love and hope in her relationship with Clym: 'She had entered the dance from the troubled hours of her late life as one might enter a brilliant chamber after a night walk in a wood'. The alliteration of 'tr' in 'tropical' and 'troubled' further highlights the difference between the dance and her life.

For Wildeve this new development is also a rebellion against social restrictions and conventions; for him the fact that both he and Eustacia are married makes his desire for her even stronger: 'Obstacles were a ripening sun to his love, and he was at this moment in a delirium of exquisite misery'. The word 'ripening' is usually applied to fruit and here suggests that his love is a forbidden fruit which tempts him to sin; their desire contravenes their Christian marriages, and their relationship is a sin in terms of Christian morality. Although both Eustacia and Wildeve are following their selfish desires, the reader is encouraged to be more critical of Wildeve. His objectification of Eustacia and his desire merely to possess what he considers belongs to another man contrasts with Eustacia's more genuine feelings, at this point, of being carried away by the excitement of the moment. The fact that the other women at the dance are likewise intoxicated encourages us not to judge her immoral behaviour too harshly (as a similar generalisation softened our criticism of Mrs Yeobright's possessive jealousy earlier, p. 251). Although Eustacia does still manipulate Wildeve later, the power balance between them seems to have shifted, and we can see that the new phase of their relationship will be different.

The scene in the moonlight, which plays a key role in producing the 'symptoms' which dangerously threaten any sense of restraint, invites comparison with the scene of Clym's proposal to Eustacia. In contrast to this earlier scene, there are crowds of people, not a deserted heath, the moon is a 'disc', not eclipsed, and Eustacia is in a 'cloud', not preoccupied with things that may hinder her ambition. However, the **simile** likening her to 'the planet Mercury surrounded by the lustre of sunset' suggests that her passionate feelings for Wildeve will be as transient as her desire for Clym. Although it is not important that they are observed here, since they are strangers in East Egdon, the suggestion of spying, even by the inanimate 'eyes' of the musical instruments, recalls Venn's spying and anticipates his further observation and intervention in their renewed relationship.

PART FIVE

Background

Thomas Hardy – Life and Works

Thomas Hardy was born in Higher Brockhampton, a village near Dorchester in Dorset, in 1840. At this time Dorset was one of the poorest counties in England, and was fairly isolated (in fact, the railways which were rapidly being built all over the country only reached Dorchester in the late 1840s). It had gained a reputation for being backward and uncouth given the violent local response to the agricultural revolution (rick-burning, machine breaking and riots) in the 1830s. Although Thomas Hardy's family was relatively prosperous – his father was a successful builder and master mason – he was aware of the hardship suffered by many of the rural poor. There was a strong sense of community and the Hardys were socially active; Thomas Hardy's father, grandfather and uncle were members of the local choir and Thomas Hardy frequently accompanied his father when he played the violin at weddings and other festivities, including mumming plays. Thomas Hardy was quite a sickly and solitary child, and he spent much of his time with adults, absorbing many of the sensational stories, folktales and local history as he listened to relatives and their friends telling their vivid tales in their local dialect.

Thomas Hardy's mother suffered great hardship in her youth and was ambitious for both her husband and her eldest son. Like Mrs Yeobright in *The Return of the Native*, Jemima Hardy wanted her son to have a professional career and saw education as the key to this. She taught him to read by the time he was three and, an avid reader herself, she continued to encourage his love of literature, giving him copies of Dryden's *Virgil* and Johnson's *Rasselas*. His first formal education was at the village school and later, in 1850, he attended Dorchester British School. Jemima paid additional fees for him to learn Latin, a subject crucial for a professional career at this time.

Although Thomas Hardy aspired to go to university or to join the Church, at sixteen he was apprenticed to a local ecclesiastical architect, John Hicks. He continued to study Greek and Latin whilst he was training, and his intellectual ambitions were encouraged through his contact with the family of the Reverend Henry Moule, the vicar of Fordington. His long-lasting friendship with the fourth son and Oxbridge scholar, Horace, was especially close. His acquaintance with the Reverend William Barnes, a teacher, philosopher and dialect poet was important, and Thomas Hardy later edited a collection of Barnes's poetry in 1908 by way of preserving and offering a translation of the Dorsetshire dialect.

In 1862, when he had completed his architectural training, Thomas Hardy went to London to pursue his career in Arthur Blomfield's architectural practice. Although he was successful as an architect, literature became increasingly important to him. He heard Charles Dickens's public readings, and read the work of other contemporary novelists, as well as the bold and independent poetry of Algernon Charles Swinburne. Life in the capital city also brought him into contact with radical theories which were challenging traditional ways of thinking. Like many other Victorian intellectuals he began to doubt his religious faith and was influenced by the ideas of cultural and scientific thinkers, for instance John Ruskin's *Modern Painters* (1843–60) and Charles Darwin's the *Origin of Species* (1859) had an impact on his thinking. His wide reading also acquainted him with the ideas of philosophers and agnostics, such as John Stuart Mill (political philosopher and MP for Westminster), Auguste Comte (founder of the theory of Positivism), Herbert Spencer (leading theorist of social evolution), and Thomas Huxley (distinguished biologist and defender of Darwinian theory). Later he was also influenced by the ideas of Arthur Schopenhauer and Matthew Arnold.

In 1867 Thomas Hardy became ill and returned to Dorset to work for Hicks again. Although he had not been successful in getting some of his poetry published whilst in London, he remained determined to fulfil his literary ambitions and finished his first semi-autobiographical novel *The Poor Man and the Lady* in 1868. It was rejected by several publishers, unsurprisingly given its social satire, attacks on Christianity and political criticism, but Thomas Hardy received an interview and vital advice from the well-known poet, George Meredith. He suggested Thomas Hardy wrote a more conventional novel with a strongly developed plot. The result, *Desperate Remedies*, again proved too unconventional, however, and Hardy published it anonymously and at his own expense in 1871.

This novel adopts some of the typical features of sensation fiction, such as the fear of discovery of a secret, illegitimate child, unconventional sexual relationships and seduction, coincidence and prophetic dreams.

Meanwhile, Thomas Hardy had met his wife-to-be, Emma Gifford; she was the daughter of the rector of St Juliot's Church and they had met when Thomas Hardy was working as an architect in Cornwall in 1870. Hardy was encouraged by the not entirely unfavourable reviews of *Desperate Remedies* and by Emma's support for his pursuit of a literary career. His next novel, *Under the Greenwood Tree: A Rural Painting of the Dutch School* was published in 1872 to great critical acclaim. However, Hardy's inexperience in dealing with shrewd publishers meant that he made little money. His next novel, *A Pair of Blue Eyes*, began to be serialised in 1872 in *Tinsley's Magazine* and like *Under the Greenwood Tree* satisfied the reading public's delight in depictions of idyllic rural life, much as George Eliot's *Adam Bede* (1859) had done earlier.

As a result of these two successes Hardy abandoned his career in architecture, a decision justified by the invitation from Leslie Stephen to write a serial for the prestigious leading journal, the *Cornhill Magazine*. *Far From the Madding Crowd* (1874) was the result, a novel which firmly established Hardy as a major writer and put his 'Wessex' on the literary map. Personally, too, it marked a massive change. His closest friend, Horace Moule, committed suicide whilst Hardy was writing it; but this loss was balanced by a positive development – now a successful and financially secure author Hardy felt able to marry Emma at last, despite her father's objection and his mother's disapproval.

Leslie Stephen requested another serial and, to resist being categorised as a rural or regional novelist, Hardy wrote *The Hand of Ethelberta*, a satire on fashionable London life and society; the reviews were largely unenthusiastic, however. Thomas Hardy was never comfortable in London and the couple left the city in 1875, eventually settling in Sturminster Newton, Dorset, in 1876. This was the happiest period of their marriage and Hardy began to plan and to write *The Return of the Native*.

This was a daring novel to write in many ways, since it was artistically ambitious and flouted conventional taste in its tragic and amoral vision of life in a landscape alien and shocking to readers with a taste for idyllic **pastorals** of rural life. It is a novel rich in **allusion** to classical Greek mythology, the Bible, Greek tragedy, Shakespeare and to the work of famous artists. This display of learned reference led to Hardy being criticised for being pretentious, and some saw his extensive use of allusion as symptomatic of his insecurity and sense of intellectual inferiority. *The Return of the Native* also has semi-autobiographical elements, not least Hardy's acknowledged reference to his own mother's sharp temper, intense love and ambition for her eldest son, and her hostility towards Emma in his depiction of Mrs Yeobright. Clym's name, Clement, is one traditional in Hardy's family and Clym in many ways expresses Thomas Hardy's feelings about city life and his attachment to the place of his birth. The very different personalities and ambitions of Clym and Eustacia may also be a reflection on Thomas Hardy's relationship with Emma, which was already showing some signs of strain.

Hardy found it difficult to find a publisher and only Mary Braddon, the sensation novelist and editor of the *Belgravia* magazine, was prepared to publish it, although Hardy was forced to modify some of its more extreme elements. It began to be serialised in January 1878 in Britain and simultaneously in *Harper's New Monthly Magazine* in America. In March, the Hardys returned to London again, so that Hardy could research the Napoleonic War for his next novel, *The Trumpet Major* (1880), and so that Emma could socialise. Hardy wrote and published several short stories in the three years that they remained in London. He took part in London's literary social life and became acquainted with several influential publishers, critics and thinkers, including Edmund Gosse, Charles Kegan Paul and Matthew Arnold. Once again Hardy became ill in London, this time very seriously, but was financially and professionally obliged to finish writing *A Laodicean. A Story of Today* (1881) with Emma acting as his amanuensis.

The Hardys returned to Dorset in 1881, and settled in Dorchester in 1883, moving to Max Gate, the house Hardy designed himself, in 1885. Although the couple travelled to Europe and spent each spring in London, the permanent move to Dorset was beneficial to Hardy's writing, since it meant a closer association with the local traditions, customs and values, and a closer proximity to his family and the home of his childhood. His essay 'The Dorsetshire Labourer' was published in *Longman's Magazine* in 1883 and publicises the dire working conditions and desperate suffering of the poor in Dorset. *Two on a Tower* began to be serialised in 1881, and in 1886 *The Mayor of Casterbridge* was also serialised and published as a novel. Hardy's own favourite novel, *The Woodlanders*, was published in 1887, and his collections of short stories, *Wessex Tales* and *A Group of Noble Dames*, were published in 1888 and 1891, respectively. It was in 1891, at the peak of his fame, that he published the shocking *Tess of the d'Urbervilles: A Pure Woman*. Readers were duly outraged by its **plot**, which revolves around a probable rape, an illegitimate birth and adultery, and especially by Hardy's defence of Tess as a 'pure woman', as the subtitle highlights. *The Well-Beloved*, which was serialised in 1892 as *The Pursuit of the Well-Beloved* in *Illustrated London News* (published as a novel in 1897) was not so rebellious, but was similarly received. However, it was *Jude the Obscure*, which was serialised between 1894–5 under the title 'Hearts Insurgent' in *Harper's Magazine* and published in novel form in 1898, which with its radical depiction of marriage and the divorce laws caused a massive furore. After this Hardy planned to give up his career as a novelist. He began to concentrate on his poetry, although he continued to write short stories and published *A Changed Man and Other Tales* in 1913. His *Wessex Poems* was published in 1898, *Poems of the Past and Present* in 1902, and *The Dynasts*, his verse-play about the Napoleonic Wars, was published in three parts between 1903 and 1908.

As a counter to this fame, the Hardys became increasingly estranged; their very different personalities proved incompatible and, following Emma's unenthusiastic response to *Jude*, they lived virtually separate lives. Some critics and biographers speculate that Hardy's increasing pessimism and tragic mode of writing had its source in the failure of his marriage and the disappointment of not having children. Although Hardy held unconventional views on marriage, believing that couples should not stay together if they were not suited, he did remain with Emma until she died in November 1912. He remarried in February 1914. His new wife, Florence Dugdale, was almost forty years his junior and had worked for Hardy as his assistant for a number of years. However, Emma's death affected Hardy deeply and in March 1913 he returned to Cornwall, revisiting the places of their courtship. He wrote many beautiful poems, 'Poems of 1912–13', which reflect on their relationship; they were published in the collection *Satires of Circumstance* (1914).

Hardy's poetry continued to win him acclaim and popularity; he refused a knighthood, but in 1910 he received the distinction of the Order of Merit and was made a Freeman of Dorchester. He also received five honorary doctorates from British universities, and honorary fellowships at Cambridge and Oxford. Although Thomas Hardy lived a quiet life at Max Gate with Florence, amongst his acquaintance in his later years were a number of influential writers, including Virginia Woolf, Siegfried Sassoon and H.G. Wells. During the last years of his life he wrote his biography which omitted information about his parents, his childhood, his early love-life and his first marriage. It was published posthumously in Florence's name in 1928 and 1930. He died in January 1928; his ashes were buried in Poet's Corner in Westminster Abbey and his heart in Emma's grave in Stinsford churchyard.

HISTORICAL BACKGROUND

MATERIAL AND POLITICAL

The nineteenth century was a time of great upheaval in all realms of life: economic, scientific, technological, social, political and cultural. In the first part of the century the agricultural and industrial revolutions radically transformed the practices and patterns of work for the majority of the population. Finding that machines had made their labour redundant, masses of rural workers were forced to migrate to the urban areas to find work in the new factories. The rapid and unplanned expansion of cities (by 1841 almost half of the population of England and Wales lived in cities) created many problems and reforms, which attempted to improve the working and living conditions of the working classes, were passed throughout the century.

Leading thinkers stressed the need to improve the lot of the majority of people and to increase equality by means of legislation. Unprecedented educational reforms took place during the century and the working classes derived some benefit from this. Although the Factories Act of 1833 entailed the setting up of factory schools and the Government gave a grant for the establishment of a network of elementary schools in the same year, it was only after Forster's

Elementary Education Act in 1870 and the 1880 Education Act that education of a consistent standard became universally available and was made compulsory for all children. *The Return of the Native* draws on the early attempts to extend educational opportunities to all classes in the 1840s with Clym's intention of setting up a school for the heath folk. Clym's perception of the necessity of this is based on fact; as Hardy was well aware, the majority of Dorset labourers were still uneducated at this time. Clym wants to be 'a schoolmaster to the poor and ignorant, to teach them what nobody else will' (p. 233). Educational reforms did bring change to this isolated area and the first school that Hardy attended was run by the National Society for Promoting the Education of the Poor in the Principles of the Established Church.

Thomas Hardy's focus in the majority of his novels is on rural life. Although he romanticised the countryside in his creation of a **pastoral** idyll in *Under the Greenwood Tree*, the majority of his fiction depicts the lives of the Dorsetshire rural poor, who were judged to be the 'most wretched of all the labouring classes'. He often draws comic stereotypes of rural folk (Grandfer and Christian Cantle in *The Return of the Native*, for example), but does not belittle their lives. *Tess of the d'Urbervilles* demonstrates the struggle to survive, and the hard labour of furze-cutting plays a key role in *The Return of the Native*. Thomas Hardy's class consciousness and his representation of rural hardship in Dorsetshire has its urban parallel in the fiction of writers who explored the suffering of the poorest in the industrial cities, for example, Elizabeth Gaskell's *Mary Barton: A Tale of Manchester Life* (1848). However, Hardy was also concerned by the loss of the local customs and the sense of regional identity as economic changes transformed agricultural workers into an undifferentiated mass of labourers, and the 'civilising' impulses of the bourgeois 'thinking world' obliterated the traditions of Dorset. Thomas Hardy was keen to preserve a record of local customs and traditions, as well as the local folk history and superstition, which continued to inform the lives of the inhabitants of Dorsetshire even in the 1890s. The inclusion of a reddleman and a discussion of his trade and place in Wessex superstition, the mummers' play of St George, the Bonfire Night and Maypole festivities, and the descriptions of the heath's flora and fauna in *The Return of the Native* demonstrate this intention.

THOUGHT AND BELIEF

During the nineteenth century there was a massive transformation in how people thought and what they believed. Scientific theories contested the religious certainties that formed the basis of belief, moral values and cultural assumptions for the majority of people in Britain. In particular, Christian notions of origin, the acceptance of the Bible as a historical record, and the belief in the existence of an omnipotent creator were violently undermined. Charles Hennell's *An Inquiry into the Origins of Christianity* (1838) was a ground-breaking study which considered the Gospels as primarily mythical writing. German intellectuals similarly challenged traditional Christianity by disentangling biblical history from its mythical elements. George Eliot's translations of David Friedrich Strauss's *Life of Jesus* (1846) and of Ludwig Feuerbach's *Essence of Christianity* (1854) significantly helped to undermine orthodox Christianity.

Charles Darwin's monumentally influential work *Origin of Species* was published in 1859. Darwin's *Descent of Man* (1871) proved even more contentious than the *Origin of Species* since it proposed that humanity's social and spiritual qualities also evolved from animals. For many Victorians the premise that morality, social tendencies and spirituality originate in animal instincts was disturbing. In general, theories of evolution permeated all aspects of Victorian culture and were 'imaginatively powerful', as Gillian Beer demonstrates in her detailed and illuminating discussion in *Darwin's Plots: Evolutionary Narrative in Darwin, George Eliot and Nineteenth-Century Fiction* (Ark Paperbacks, 1983).

Hardy's own preoccupations with genealogy and heredity initially predisposed him to accept Darwinian ideas. The evolutionary concerns with origin, heredity, and an emphasis on kinship and environment are key issues in *The Return of the Native*. The emphasis that evolutionary theories place on chance and extinction are similarly important features of the novel's plot. Critics have claimed that Hardy's use of coincidence is too contrived. However, in his use of frequent chance meetings and happenings Hardy is not only emphasising the small and isolated space that his characters inhabit, but seems also to be exploring evolutionary ideas, as well as the fatalistic perception of life typical of the natives of Dorsetshire. The heath itself is like some kind of primordial landscape, and seems timeless and unchanging: 'To many persons this Egdon was a place which had slipped out of its century generations ago, to intrude as an uncouth object into this. It was an obsolete thing, and few cared to study it' (p. 232). The choice of 'study', meaning 'to look at' here, also carries the suggestion of Egdon being a site for scientific study.

However, Darwinism was not a source of optimism for Hardy. The fates of his characters suggest that survival is not the only measure of value, and that even the most aspiring can be defeated. Clym struggles to achieve a higher kind of human life and is defeated. Hardy seems to express Clym's ambitions in terms of Lamarck's theory of evolution (proposed at the beginning of the nineteenth century) where will, intention and habit can generate improvement. But the main drive of the novel insists on a more Darwinian concept of development in which human will is ineffectual in the face of the natural forces of the heath. Further, Hardy suggests that these forces are malign, that the natural laws are defective and put humans in a 'quandary' (p. 225). Clym hopes to bring progress to the heath with his new 'system of education', seemingly influenced by the ideas of the leading French socialist thinkers of the 1830s and 1840s, Saint-Simon and Comte, and of British thinkers, Carlyle and Ruskin. However, his scheme is not allowed to develop; after his blindness Clym is seemingly absorbed into the heath and his reforming zeal dissipates. Indeed, Hardy seems pessimistic that any 'system' would be adequate to explain human suffering. Time on Egdon Heath is collapsed so that ancient beliefs coexist with Christianity and with the more modern secular systems of belief based on scientific explanation of the world. None it seems can ameliorate the agonies of life on this earth, and significantly in his role as an itinerant preacher Clym abandons 'creeds and systems of philosophy' (p. 474).

Hardy has often been criticised for his depiction of female characters who transgress what is considered socially acceptable behaviour for women, as well as for representing scandalously unconventional male-female relationships. The ideas of John Stuart Mill and John Ruskin (two of the most influential and radically opposed nineteenth-century thinkers on these issues) seem to have influenced Hardy's work. In many ways Hardy's representations of women, marriage and sexual relationships between men and women seem to be informed by Mill's ideas, expressed in his 1869 essay 'The Subjection of

Women' (in *On Liberty, Representative Government and the Subjection of Women: Three Essays by John Stuart Mill*, first published 1912, Oxford University Press). Mill argues that a woman's role within marriage is worse than that of a slave; he questions what is natural and argues that the inferiority attributed to women is merely customary or socially constructed. He adds that preventing over half of the population from attaining their potential is detrimental to human society as a whole.

However, Thomas Hardy also seems to express Ruskin's very different ideas about women as guardians of morality (see Ruskin's essay 'Of Queens' Gardens', published in *Sesame and Lilies and the Political Economy of Art*, 1865). The ending of *The Return of the Native* seems to punish Eustacia for being rebellious and immoral, and for transgressing the conventional social role that Ruskin valorises. However, the moral message is made equivocal by the narrator's ambiguous attitude to her behaviour and by the fact that we are increasingly made to feel sympathy for her. Similarly the good woman Thomasin, who adheres to what Ruskin calls woman's 'separate sphere' of domesticity, marriage and motherhood is rewarded with another chance at romance. However, the moral message of this is also made uncertain since this ending seems too formulaic and anti-climactic given the emotional intensity of the rest of the novel.

LITERARY BACKGROUND

At the time that Thomas Hardy was writing, literary production was a flourishing business. The burgeoning of the middle classes (who comprised the majority of novel readers), improving standards of literacy with educational reforms, and increasing access to fiction via serial publication in family and literary magazines, as well as via Charles Edward Mudie's circulating libraries, created a boom in demand for fiction. This growth also gave rise to an increasing diversification in the form of the novel as sub-genres (such as the social-problem novel, the Utopian novel, the sensation novel, and the school novel) were developed to cater to the varied tastes of the reading public.

However, the values and prejudices of the middle-class reading public had an impact on the choice of subjects writers could explore; the idea that literature should be morally edifying became increasingly important in the 1860s and 1870s. The sway that readers could have owed much to the means of distribution of fiction: if serials were not popular and circulation of the magazines decreased writers were asked to modify their stories accordingly; similarly, if Mudie, who 'acted as an unofficial defender of public morals', and his customers took offence at a novel it could be withdrawn with potentially disastrous consequences for the writer (Michael Wheeler, *English Fiction of the Victorian Period 1830–1890*, 1985, p. 2).

Thomas Hardy was one writer who especially felt constrained by such censorship and control. In his essay 'Candour in Fiction' (1890) Hardy attacks the direct and indirect censorship which limited a writer's creativity and sincerity, and which prevented the representation of more truthful relationships between men and women. *The Return of the Native* is perhaps a unique case in the history of revision and bowdlerisation. His serial version was revised for publication as a three volume novel in 1878; many of the anti-Christian elements were removed, the social status of Clym and Eustacia was elevated and the issues of adultery and elopement remained suppressed. Hardy's revision in the third version of the novel, published in the quite different cultural climate of 1895, reconstructed the novel quite radically. It raised the social status of Clym and Eustacia still further and made clear Eustacia and Wildeve's adultery and attempt to elope. Finally, for the Wessex Edition of 1912 Hardy once again gave the relationship of Eustacia and Wildeve an element of ambiguity. It was in this edition of the novel that Hardy's resentment of the necessity of meeting the demands of his readers is expressed (in his footnote to Book Sixth, p. 464). The starkness of his original conception would not have been acceptable to either publishers or readers in the nineteenth century, who preferred a happy ending as a reinforcement of a moral message. However, in the literary climate of the early twentieth century readers may well have chosen the more 'austere' conclusion to be the one more consistent' and 'true' (p. 464).

In many ways Thomas Hardy's writing exhibits features more typical of twentieth-century fiction than those which predominate in Victorian novels. A pessimistic vision of life with the recognition of the hopelessness of existence and a wish not to live, coupled with a sense of existential alienation and loneliness in a hostile or indifferent universe add a distinctively modern tone to Hardy's fiction. The sense of social dislocation that Hardy's characters often feel contrasts with the social realism in the writing of his contemporaries, such as Anthony Trollope and William Thackeray.

However, Hardy's fiction is also in many ways typically Victorian. His *Far From the Madding Crowd* was at first mistakenly assumed to be written by the most pre-eminent of the Victorian realist writers, George Eliot. However, unlike the work of many realist novelists, Hardy's fiction is not didactic and does not offer a clear moral message. Many critics have noted the duality of **realism** and **Romanticism** which characterises much Victorian writing, and in this respect Hardy's fiction is typical. *The Return of the Native* attempts to give a realistic representation of rural life, but also emphasises the importance of Nature, and has poetic and mythical qualities which align it with the Romantic mode of writing associated with novelists such as Sir Walter Scott. Like the Romantic poet, William Wordsworth, Hardy focused on the lives of ordinary individuals, and allowed his characters to speak in their native dialect, using what Wordsworth called 'the language of men' (1800 Preface to *Lyrical Ballads*, by William Wordsworth and Samuel Taylor Coleridge, R.L. Brett and A.R. Jones, eds, Methuen, 1963, pp. 244–5).

Also, following George Meredith's advice, Hardy adopted some of the features of the popular sensation novels of the time, such as Wilkie Collins's *The Woman in White* (1860), *The Moonstone* (1868) and Mary Braddon's *Lady Audley's Secret* (1862). Illegitimacy (of children, relationships and behaviour) characterise this genre, as do secrets, coincidence and chance, prophetic dreams, misdirected or unreceived letters, intense emotions and suspense. Many of these features can be identified in *The Return of the Native*, although Hardy did not attempt a wholly sensational novel after the relative failure of *Desperate Remedies*.

PART SIX

CRITICAL HISTORY & BROADER PERSPECTIVES

RECEPTION AND EARLY REVIEWS

The Return of the Native received a mixed and sometimes contradictory response from critics. Typically, Hardy's descriptions of nature were praised and his style criticised.

As with *Far From the Madding Crowd*, critics found the dialogue of the rural folk unfeasibly sophisticated, although the *Spectator* did find their talk 'most amusing and original' as well (unsigned review, February 1879, in Cox, p. 56). In general, the earliest reviews and criticism found Hardy's characters unconvincing, unrealistic and somewhat mechanical, although some critics, W.E. Henley for example, found them to be 'of value and of interest' *(Academy*, November 1878, in Cox, p. 49). The majority of critics were disparaging about the sense of **tragedy** in the novel, finding it 'arbitrary and accidental rather than heroic and inevitable' (Henley in the *Academy*, in Cox, p. 48). His characters, compared to Shakespeare's tragic figures, were considered to be unconvincing and unsuited to such a mode of writing.

However, *The Return of the Native* sold well and was widely praised for its originality and powerful descriptions. One of the first general surveys of Hardy's fiction praised the primary role he gave to his female characters, and hailed Hardy as 'a new genius' (unsigned survey in the *New Quarterly Magazine*, October 1879, in Cox, p. 60). *The Return of the Native* was seen as a turning point in Hardy's career, the novel 'presents a new phase, and perhaps a new departure in the development of Mr. Hardy's genius' (ibid. p. 67).

R.G. Cox, ed., *Thomas Hardy: The Critical Heritage*, Routledge and Kegan Paul, 1970

Contains a good range of early reviews and criticism

R.P. Draper, ed., *Thomas Hardy. The Tragic Novels*, Macmillan, 1975 (revised edition 1991)

Contains extracts from Hardy's *The Life of Thomas Hardy* and from his essays 'The Dorsetshire Labourer' and 'Candour in English Fiction', as well as a range twentieth-century critical comments and essays

Thomas Hardy received a steady and increasing amount of critical attention as his reputation grew not only in Britain and America, but also in Europe as his work was translated. Early reviews and critical essays praised Hardy's representations of rural life and his powers of description, but criticised the more sensational and improbable aspects of his **plots**, and commented on what was perceived to be an unevenness, or even clumsiness, of style. His fiction was compared (often unfavourably) with that of George Eliot and Wilkie Collins. Later, critics were concerned with Hardy's pessimistic vision, and the issues of morality and philosophy that his fiction raised. In general, however, there was a great variety of opinion and a range of often conflicting views on each novel.

One long and detailed essay in the *Westminster Review* in 1883 was written by the leading psychologist Havelock Ellis. Ellis suggests that what distinguishes Hardy as a novelist is his depiction of rural characters, his new 'intensely original' insights into nature, and the psychological aspects of his female characters (in Cox, p. 120). The leading critic Edmund Gosse also commented on Hardy's unconventional female characters: 'Mr. Hardy's women are moulded of the same flesh as his men' (in Cox, p. 170). Hardy's more realistic representation Gosse calls 'feminine realism', although he also suggests that many women readers object to such representation which is so unlike the flattering but 'practically inhuman type' of women conventionally found in novels of the period (in Cox, pp. 169–70).

In the 1890s the first book-length studies began to appear. Early twentieth-century critics drew attention to Hardy's pessimism and use of **irony**, and to his creation of atmosphere; he was perceived as a great tragic artist, his fiction being compared with Greek drama. D.H. Lawrence *(Study of Thomas Hardy*, 1914) and Virginia Woolf (*The Novels of Thomas Hardy*, 1928) reappraised aspects of his fiction which were earlier perceived as flaws – his style, breaks with **realism**, his creation of **tragedy**, and his **characterisation**. For Lawrence and Woolf, Hardy's characterisation is a highly distinctive aspect of his fiction. Lawrence discusses the unpredictability of Hardy's characters, their struggle to free themselves from social conventions which imprison and restrict them, and ultimately their explosion out of such conventions which results in their destruction. This forms a consistent pattern in Hardy's fiction.

For Woolf, the three or four main characters of each novel 'stand up like lightening conductors to attract the force of the elements', and their intense passions make them memorable (in Draper, p. 74). She claims that Hardy has sympathy for his characters, especially for his female characters who, although they are 'weaker and fleshlier' and 'cling' to the stronger male characters, are treated with a 'more tender solicitude' than the male characters (in Draper, p. 74). Woolf here anticipates the ambiguities in later **feminist** criticisms of Hardy's fiction.

David Cecil's highly influential *Hardy the Novelist* (1943) reiterates the idea that Hardy is a great tragic writer whose work is stylistically flawed and stresses Hardy's Englishness. In the 1950s there was a trend of sociological critical approaches to Hardy's writing which perceive him as a rural annalist, documenting the changes in rural life. Douglas Brown's *Thomas Hardy* (1954) is one of the most influential and traces a strong sense of the relation between the work, society and economy of Victorian rural England. He sees Hardy as mourning the decline of rural communities as industrialisation disrupts the natural peace of the countryside.

Albert J. Guerard's *Thomas Hardy: The Novels and Stories* (1949) made a break to a certain extent with the firmly entrenched trends in Hardy criticism. He argues that Hardy's inclusion of improbability, coincidence, macabre and supernatural elements, **irony**, myth and sexuality was not a flaw but a deliberate break with realism. He also explores Hardy's concern with class, and was perhaps the first to shift critical attention onto the psychological aspects of Hardy's fiction. The 1960s and 1970s saw a greater diversification of critical approaches which also tackle these issues from **formalist, structuralist, psychoanalytical, deconstructionist, Marxist** and **feminist** perspectives.

Ian Gregor's formalist reading of Hardy's major novels suggests that the structure of Hardy's major fiction, with its patterns, parallel scenes, coincidences and allusion, functions as a **metaphor** for Hardy's vision of life. For instance, Gregor argues that the inconclusiveness of the ending of *The Return of the Native* in the final version (which retains both the conventional happy ending demanded by earlier audiences and Hardy's apparently preferred 'artistically true' ending in the footnote) dramatises Hardy's uncertainty about what constitutes an appropriate ending (Gregor 1974, pp. 104–5). Dale Kramer (1975) argues that the structure of Hardy's novels is inextricably linked to the development of tragedy.

The deconstructionist critic J. Hillis Miller (1970) argues that the motifs of distance and desire form a connection between theme and structure in Hardy's fiction. The dualism of detachment and attachment, expressed in the contrasts between the real and the ideal which recur throughout Hardy's writing, forms a 'deep structure' or underlying pattern. Peter J. Casagrande (1982), similarly analyses the structure of Hardy's fiction. He identifies repeated motifs and patterns of return and restoration, and traces these patterns in Hardy's oeuvre as a whole, arguing that there are 'antecedents' and 'rehearsals' of the major novels in the early or minor novels. He also identifies similar character types, of which Clym is a 'nostalgic idealist' along with Angel Clare in *Tess* and Sue Bridehead in *Jude* (Casagrande, p. 2, p. 5).

Casagrande also makes use of biographical material in his analysis, seeing *The Return of the Native* as 'thinly veiled autobiography', linking it to Hardy's relationships with his mother and his wife (p. 126). He suggests that '[t]he story of return was a deeply personal one for Hardy' and is inextricably linked to his identity as a novelist, since Hardy's literary success is largely due to his imaginative recreation of the landscape of his childhood, and his literal return to Dorset stimulates his literary creativity and productivity (p. 5). He argues that the theme of Hardy's novels is always that 'there is no return, no restoration' (p. 2). Clym returns to the heath, but is not restored to his mother or reinstated into the community of the heath folk. Instead 'he ends as a mother-obsessed son' (p. 133) and his homecoming is 'destructive' and 'unnatural' (p. 127). Drawing parallels between Clym and the unusual 'children' in the novel (Johnny Nunsuch and Christian Cantle), Casagrande argues that Clym's return is also a sign of his sexual immaturity (pp. 134–5).

Other critics have also considered the psychological aspects of Hardy's fiction. *The Return of the Native* readily lends itself to psychoanalytic critical approaches with its inclusion of prophetic dreams. Egdon Heath functions as a metaphor for an indifferent universe, but can also be interpreted as a psychological landscape. The heath can be seen to reflect the internal chaos of the characters and to represent the primitive and instinctive aspects of human nature. Rosemary Sumner (1981) argues that Hardy's psychological insights and imaginative exploration of repressed desires anticipate the early twentieth-century developments in psychology, in the work of Sigmund Freud and Carl Jung.

More recently, Robert Langbaum (1995) sees the heath as a **symbol** of the unconscious as well as representing 'the maternal principle' (p. 95). He interprets Clym's return to the heath as an unconscious return to his mother and sees Clym's relationship with his mother as implicitly incestuous, as is suggested by Hardy's references to the Greek tragedy of Oedipus in which Oedipus unwittingly marries his mother, Jocasta, and blinds himself when he discovers his sin. Mrs Yeobright's attempts to deter Clym from marrying her rival Eustacia also **alludes** to Sophocles' drama through the reference to blindness. Metaphorical references to a lack of light as a result of Clym's sinning against his mother suggest that his mother's death does leave him emotionally and psychologically blinded (Langbaum, p. 101).

Issues of class and ideology in Hardy's writing have been discussed by critics taking a **Marxist** approach. For example, Raymond Williams (1970) considers the pressures and strains on Hardy's writing which stem from his ambiguous social position. He interprets Hardy's writing in the light of the novelist's uncertainty about his class position, and the fact that his education and social mobility cut him off from his origins. Hardy's perception of his native communities and their history and traditions is a double one: 'He sees as a participant who is also an observer; this is the source of the strain. For the process which allows him to observe [education] is very clearly in Hardy's time one which includes, in its attachment to class feelings and class separations, a decisive alienation' (Williams, p. 90). William's argues that Hardy's style, with its mixture of 'Latinism', scientific discourse, and simpler modes of writing, is also affected by his education and his ambiguous class position as both an insider and an outsider to the middle-class literary world (p. 89). He notes the centrality and importance of work in Hardy's fiction and sees Clym as exemplifying Hardy's understanding of the complex process of historical change which means that education is inextricably linked to social advancement.

Later Marxist criticism has been influenced by **Structuralism, Post-structuralism** and **Feminism**. The prominent Marxist critic Terry Eagleton engages with such theoretical influences in his comments on

Hardy (1976 and 1987). Eagleton argues that what bourgeois critics label as Hardy's flaws (his unevenness of style, mixing of literary forms, pessimism, fatalism, sensationalism and improbabilities) are an open defiance of Victorian conventions and an exposure of the ideological inconsistencies and impossibilities that Victorian fiction usually glosses over. Peter Widdowson (1989) writing from a Marxist theoretical perspective undertakes the comprehensive project of reinterpreting or critically reconstructing Hardy in a way which presents him as a subversive writer. He develops the arguments of Williams and Eagleton, and illustrates Hardy's class ambiguity by arguing that although Hardy was a professional literary man and he moved in middle-class intellectual circles, he also wrote in a way which offended middle-class Victorian values. Widdowson stresses the class consciousness evident in Hardy's fiction: 'without exception they [the novels] hinge on class relations, on individuals' uncertainties as to what class or class faction they belong to, or on the problems of a radical shift in class position' (p. 205). In *The Return of the Native* 'the social location of its main characters' is 'scrupulously specific' (p. 208). He suggests that the 'matrix of all of Hardy's ironic "tragedies of modern life"' is 'a class society which arbitrarily discriminates human beings by the artifice of social status' and which operates to 'destroy individual aspiration by way of social mechanisms that dispossess people through the fiction of superiority/inferiority' (p. 207).

He argues, as does Eagleton, that Hardy **deconstructs** the **realist** mode in order to expose the limits of realist writing and to depict 'the real social forces, pressures, contradictions, and exploitations within which individuals actually live out their lives' (p. 74). Widdowson also introduces a consideration of the gender politics in Hardy's fiction as a further complication of Hardy's representation of class and social mobility. His female characters are generally more upwardly socially mobile than his male characters, which conveys 'the sense is of women as a dynamically emergent social group' and as 'the most potentially destabilising force' (p. 215). However, the 'gender-biased class society' also oppresses women more forcefully (p. 215) and Widdowson suggests that the logic of Hardy's texts, which mostly destroys or contains women's aspirations, may represent Hardy's fear of women and their social mobility, and be a result of Hardy's own class insecurities (pp. 217–8).

Hardy's writing has from the outset attracted conflicting attention from **feminist** critics who see it as either endorsing sexist and stereotypical images of and attitudes to women, or as radically subverting Victorian conventions and the double moral standard. Since the 1960s the development of feminist perspectives on Hardy has been a fruitful source of critical reassessment and attention has focused on social analysis, gender politics, and his disruption of the realist mode of writing.

John Bayley, *An Essay on Hardy*, Cambridge University Press, 1978

Douglas Brown, *Thomas Hardy*, Longman, 1954
    Considers the historical accuracy of Hardy's fiction

Jean Brooks, *Thomas Hardy: The Poetic Structure*, Elek Books, London, 1971

Peter Casagrande, *Unity in Hardy's Novels: 'Repetitive Symmetries'*, Macmillan, 1982

David Cecil, *Hardy the Novelist*, Constable, London, 1943

Terry Eagleton, *Criticism and Ideology. A Study in Marxist Literary Theory*, New Left Books, 1976

Terry Eagleton, *Walter Benjamin or Towards a Revolutionary Criticism*, Verso, London, 1987

Ian Gregor, *The Great Web: The Form of Hardy's Major Fiction*, Faber, 1974

Albert J. Guerard, *Thomas Hardy. The Novels and Stories*, Cambridge, Massachusetts, 1949

J. Hillis Miller, *Thomas Hardy: Distance and Desire*, Oxford University Press, 1970

Dale Kramer, *Thomas Hardy: The Forms of Tragedy*, 1975

Robert Langbaum, *Thomas Hardy in Our Time*, Macmillan, 1995

John Paterson, *The Making of 'The Return of the Native'*, University of California Press, 1960
    Uncovers the various and dramatic changes made to this text from the manuscript to the final published version

Rosemary Sumner, *Thomas Hardy: Psychological Novelist*, 1981

Peter Widdowson, *Hardy in History: A Study in Literary Sociology*, Routledge, 1989

Merryn Williams in *Thomas Hardy and Rural England*, 1972

Raymond Williams, *The English Novel from Dickens to Lawrence*, Chatto and Windus, 1970

SOME CONTEMPORARY APPROACHES

MARXIST APPROACHES

Since the 1960s **Marxist criticism** has been influenced by European theoretical developments and George Wotton's *Thomas Hardy: Towards a Materialist Criticism* (1985) is written from a Marxist perspective influenced by **Post-structuralism** and **Feminism**. Like Widdowson in *Hardy in History: A Study in Literary Sociology*, Wotton engages with issues of class and gender, and explores the relations between history, ideology, writing and criticism. He sees history as 'a dynamic on-going process' (p. 15) and his explicit aim is to 'historicise' Hardy's writing, not in order to see how Hardy's writing reflects history, but to see it as 'a social event'. He explores the way that Hardy's writing functions 'in the process of cultural/ideological production' as well as 'in reproducing the acutal relations of production in class society' (preface, pages not numbered).

Wotton argues that Hardy's 'aesthetic project' (the ideological effect he intends his writing to have) is the production of an insight into the realities of life. The richly complex imaginary world Hardy creates resembles, but does not reflect, the real world; however, it does allow knowledge and insight to be gained from how this world is perceived. He argues that:

> the real social contradictions in class society are transformed into problems of individual perception. Class struggle is idealized into conflicting points of view, sights and oversights in vision, everything becoming a matter of the individual subject's true or false acts of seeing. Thus in Hardy's writing class and gender conflicts appear as conflicts of perception in the multifarious acts of seeing of the characters who inhabit Wessex. (pp. 3–4)

In particular, Wotton sees Hardy as being preoccupied with the destruction of Dorsetshire traditions that economic changes and the civilising impulse of the 'thinking world' bring. Wotton argues that Eustacia, alone on the barrow and gazing out over the heath at the beginning of the novel, represents the 'harmonising' discourse and the civilising impulses of the 'thinking world' (which smooth over the conflicts of capitalism and a class society, promote a sense of universal freedom and progress, and threaten the identity and traditions of Dorsetshire). Wotton suggests that the pre-eminence of her consciousness (as she stands on the highest point) is disrupted, however, when the heath folk intrude with their celebration and preservation of ancient traditions, and force her to leave her elevated position.

His later discussion of *The Return of the Native* continues to focus on a structure of perceptions as a means of representing class and gender conflicts. The main drive of the novel, he argues, is centred on the conflict between the two principle modes of perception – the 'intuitive' and 'idealizing' modes. Diggory Venn, Mrs Yeobright, Thomasin, and the heath folk have 'intuitive insight', which is 'a mode of perception which signifies the relationship of intimacy with, and experiential knowledge of the community of labour' (p. 114). Intuitive insight is especially emphasised by the altruism of Diggory Venn. Eustacia is the detached, distanced onlooker whose vision is idealizing; she creates her world through her idealizing perception of it. However, her idealizing vision is limited and ultimately destructive, as is seen in the shattering of her vision of Clym as her ideal lover. In contrast with Thomasin, who sees Egdon in material or practical terms, Eustacia perceives it as a nightmare world as she makes her final journey across the heath. Wotton argues that what Hardy wants the reader to see is that it is Eustacia's vision of Egdon as a prison which imprisons her, not the actual place.

Clym becomes the focus of the conflict between the two modes of perception; he is part of the heath and has intuitive vision, but also brings idealized views from the cosmopolitan and highly civilised city of Paris. These views would undermine the communal and customary modes of intuitive perception. His physically impaired vision circumscribes his socially idealizing vision and he is forced to return to physical work on the heath. In the passage which describes Clym as he watches the mumming play, the reader is meant to see in this image of him the end of a way of life, and the end of 'that structure of unity which Hardy believed his class represented', as well as the future affected by the disease of civilisation – thought (p. 120).

Wotton sums up his discussion with the assertion that the conflicting perceptions, which express class conflicts, 'produce[s] a *scenario* of the way people become conscious of the conflicts between the forces and relations of production and fight them out' (p. 121).

George Wotton, *Thomas Hardy: Towards a Materialist Criticism*, Gill and Macmillan, Ireland, 1985

John Goode, *Thomas Hardy: The Offensive Truth*, Basil Blackwell, 1988
> Argues that Hardy was not complicit with conventional opinion, but was rather critical, questioning and intentionally offensive. In the section of *The Return of the Native*, he suggests that the 'tragical possibilities' of the novel are simply a fundamental condition of human existence

FEMINIST APPROACHES

Feminists have long found Hardy to be 'an irresistible paradox' (Elaine Showalter in 'The Unmanning of the Mayor of Casterbridge', in Kramer, p. 99). Feminists have read his work as expressing conventional, sexist, antifeminist, and even misogynistic attitudes, as well as seeing evidence of proto-feminism in his unconventionally sensitive and sympathetic portrayals of female characters, who always have a central role in his fiction. Earlier feminist criticism tends to focus on Hardy's authorial intention, and perceives his images of women as reflections of the historical or realistic position of women in an oppressive **patriarchal** society. Kate Millett's reading of *Jude the Obscure* in her groundbreaking study *Sexual Politics* (1970) is an example of this. Others, Patricia Stubbs in *Women and Fiction: Feminism and the Novel 1880–1920* (1979) for instance, argue that Hardy's representations of women are contradictory, since they are both typical of Victorian patriarchal ideology, as well as subversive of conventional character types. Rosalind Miles in 'The Women of Wessex' (1979), however, sees Hardy's admiration of women's essential 'otherness' as positive.

Elaine Showalter praises Hardy as 'one of the few Victorian male novelists who wrote in what may be called a female tradition' and who displayed an understanding of men and women in human terms (in Kramer, p. 99). Like other feminist critics, she acknowledges Hardy's psychologically insightful representations of women, which evoked comparisons with some of the great women writers of the period (Charlotte Brontë and George Eliot), whilst recognising that his writing also expresses traditional views of women. Her feminist analysis then, unusually, focuses on the central male character of *The Mayor of Casterbridge*, Michael Henchard, and she explores what is repressed and lost when men assume a masculine identity. She proposes that maturity for Hardy's male characters 'involves a kind of assimilation of female suffering, an identification with a woman which is also an effort to come to terms with their own deepest selves' (in Kramer, p. 101). She also argues that Henchard's suffering and loss of the **symbols** of male authority demonstrates Hardy's rejection of typically misogynist and masculinist attitudes, and that instead he swerved towards 'his own insistent and original exploration of human motivation' (in Kramer, p. 114). A similar feminist reading of *The Return of the Native* could be applied to Clym, who seems to 'assimilate female suffering' when he replaces Eustacia on the barrow at the end. The deaths of his mother and Eustacia leave him in fear of assuming the manly role of husband that he thinks Thomasin demands of him, and his first sermon may be a warning about the destructiveness of manly behaviour when it goes against a woman's wishes.

Later feminist readings engage with **deconstructionist** and **Marxist** approaches and focus on the ideological construction of woman, and on the formal, structural and linguistic aspects of Hardy's writing. Penny Boumelha (1982), reads Hardy's fiction in the context of the Victorian ideological and iconographical polarisation of women as angel/demon, virgin/whore. She takes a **post-structuralist** approach and explores how systems of representation encode the relationships of power and dominance, and discusses Hardy's engagement with the increasing amount of public debate about female sexuality and marriage in the latter part of the century. She suggests that Hardy deals with marriage in a new way in *The Return of the Native*, where it is treated **ironically** and is central to the double **tragedy** which develops. She sees the novel as presenting conventional polarisations of men and women, however, since the male tragedy is depicted as an intellectual, moral and historically located tragedy (Clym is influenced by the 1840's French ethical systems), whereas the female tragedy is depicted as sexual and doubly ahistorical because it is presented in terms of myth and attributed to Eustacia's essential feminine nature (p. 49).

Boumelha sees a correlation between Hardy's radical and subversive representations of sexual and marital relations and his experimentation with genre and modes of narration. She suggests that in *The Return of the Native* there is a clash in terms of literary form as the realistic narrative collides with the novel's mythological scheme. Further, she argues that the three female characters are drawn using three modes of writing – the **pastoral**, the **Romantic**, and the **realistic**. Thomasin is created using the pastoral mode, which suggests her sense of harmony with her socially endorsed role as wife and mother. Eustacia is created using the Romantic mode, which expresses her physically and socially isolated existence, her Promethean rebellion and self destruction, and her powerful desires, which are threatening because 'irreconcilable' with social forms. However, Mrs Yeobright demands a realistic mode of expression in order to explore the psychological and emotional complexities of the intense and detailed description of parent-child relationship with Clym.

Focusing on the literary language and linguistic structures available to Hardy, Patricia Ingham (1989) explores the 'disjunction' or recurrent 'fault-line' in Hardy's treatment of women and femininity that many feminists have noted in his writing. The discourses available to Hardy were limited to:

> a restricted set of 'feminine' signs clustered round 'the womanly' and 'womanhood' and the generic 'woman', a narrative syntax falling into limited patterns, cast resolutely in the indicative (the mood of assertion and definition) and a delimited semantic range that excluded the erotic. (p. 12)

She analyses his female characters as 'signs' trapped in male-dominated language, syntax, ideological constructions, and narrative structures. In the early novels Ingham detects a disturbance of narrative patterns and a modification of 'signs and syntax' – the 'fault-line' feminist critics have identified – when female characters begin to perceive their difference from conventional models of femininity as positive (p. 7). In the later novels the struggle for autonomy is 'more extensive and more explicitly articulated' (p. 7) and the 'fault-line became and earthquake that shattered novelistic language' (p. 13).

Referring to Eustacia as 'a special case', Ingham explores how she is made to evade the feminine signs of 'fallen woman' and 'seductress' which would conventionally entrap her. Instead, the pagan mythological imagery with which she is constructed 'erases' the sign of the fallen woman; Hardy avoids the dichotomy of angel/fallen woman by creating Eustacia as a goddess (pp. 24–5). Considering **plot** as a narrative discourse, Ingham argues that despite being constrained by the limited narrative syntax available to him, Hardy was involved in the process of subverting such narrative patterns. The fallen woman is conventionally punished by the development of the plot; however, the deaths of Hardy's fallen women are a source of unease. Eustacia's death is surrounded by ambiguity. She does not take on the self-hatred typical of a fallen woman, and her death actually elevates her; the description of her dead body is 'artistically fitting on a visual level' and 'deeply symbolic' (p. 41). Thus Hardy's plots encode ambivalence, taking the narrative discourse to extremes and leaving the novel 'open-ended and interrogative' (pp. 27, 41).

Penny Boumelha, *Thomas Hardy and Women: Sexual Ideology and Narrative Form*, Harvester, 1982

Patricia Ingham, *Thomas Hardy*, Harvester, 1989

Rosalind Miles, 'The Women of Wessex' in *The Novels of Thomas Hardy*, ed. Anne Smith, Vision, London, 1979

Kate Millett, *Sexual Politics*, Virago, 1977 (first published 1970)

Rosemarie Morgan, *Women and Sexuality in the Novels of Thomas Hardy*, Routledge, 1988
    A very positive feminist consideration of Hardy

Elaine Showalter, 'The Unmanning of the Mayor of Casterbridge', in Dale Kramer, *Critical Approaches to the Fiction of Thomas Hardy*, Macmillan, 1979

CHRONOLOGY

World events	Hardy's life	Literary events
		1798-1844 Heyday of British Romantic Movement
		1832 Death of Sir Walter Scott
1834 Union workhouses established; transportation to Australia of Tolpuddle martyrs		**1834** Harrison Ainsworth, *Rookwood*
1837 Accession of Queen Victoria		
1838 Formation of Anti-Corn Law League		
	1839 Thomas Hardy, mason, marries Jemima, cook	
	1840 Birth of **Thomas Hardy**, their son, at Higher Bockhampton, Dorset	**1840** Birth of Emile Zola
		1844 William Barnes, *Poems of Rural Life in the Dorset Dialect*
1846 Repeal of Corn Laws		
1847 Railway comes to Dorchester		
	1848 Attends village school	**1848** Elizabeth Gaskell, *Mary Barton: A Tale of Manchester Life*
	1850 Attends Dorchester British School	**1850** Birth of Guy de Maupassant; death of Wordsworth; Nathaniel Hawthorne, *The Scarlet Letter*
1851 The Great Exhibition shows first reaping and threshing machines		
1854-6 Crimean War		
		1855 Death of Charlotte Brontë
	1856-62 Apprenticed to architect John Hicks	**1857** Gustave Flaubert, *Madame Bovary*
		1859 Charles Darwin, *On the Origin of the Species*
		1860 George Eliot, *The Mill on the Floss;* Wilkie Collins, *The Woman in White*
		1861 Charles Dickens, *Great Expectations;* George Eliot, *Silas Marner*
	1862-7 Works in London as architect; begins to lose religious faith	**1862** Mary Braddon, *Lady Audley's Secret*
		1865 John Ruskin, *Sesame and Lilies and the Political Economy of Art*
		1866 Dostoevsky, *Crime and Punishment*
	1867 Returns to Dorchester to work for Hicks; begins working on *The Poor Man and the Lady*	

CHRONOLOGY

World events	Hardy's life	Literary events
	1869 Moves to Weymouth to work for architect Crickmay; begins writing *Desperate Remedies*	**1869** J.S. Mill, *'The Subjection of Women'*
1870 Foster's Education Act; elementary education for all; from hereon depopulation of Dorset countryside; from this date county moves from general use of 3-life leases to 1-year leases	**1870** Restoring St Juliot's church, north Cornwall, Hardy meets his future wife, Emma Lavinia Gifford	
	1871 Publishes *Desperate Remedies*	**1871-2** George Eliot, *Middlemarch*
	1872 Publishes *A Pair of Green Eyes; Under the Greenwood Tree*	
	1873 *Far from the Madding Crowd* serialised	
1874-80 Disraeli Prime Minister	**1874** Marries Emma	
	1876 They go to live at Sturminster Newton; *The Hand of Ethelberta* published	
		1877 Henry James, *The American*
	1878 *The Return of the Native*	**1878** Leo Tolstoy, *Anna Karenina*
	1880 *The Trumpet Major;* very ill for six months	**1880** Richard Jefferies, *Hodge and his Masters;* Maupassant, *Boule de Suif*
	1883 'The Dorsetshire Labourer'	
1884 Foundation of Fabian Society		**1884** Jefferies, *The Dewy Morn*
1885 Siege of Khartoum		
1886 Six 'Jack the Ripper' murders, east London	**1886** *The Mayor of Casterbridge*	
	1887 *The Woodlanders*	**1887** Emile Zola, *La Terre (Earth)*
		1890 Frazer, *The Golden Bough*
1891 Education made free in England	**1891** *Tess of the d'Urbervilles*	
	1896 *Jude the Obscure*	
	1898 *Wessex Poems*	
1899-1902 Boer War		
	1904 *The Dynasts*	
	1912 Death of Emma	
1914-18 First World War	**1914** Marries Florence Emily Dugdale, his secretary	
	1928 Death of Thomas Hardy	

absurd, theatre of the absurd the condition in which all action and endeavour is perceived as ineffectual, ridiculous, even comical, taking place, according to existentialists, in a world void of purpose

alliteration a sequence of repeated consonantal sounds in a stretch of language

allusion the inclusion of passages or phrases from other literary texts, or the imitation or parody of another writer's style in order to introduce implicit contrasts or comparisons

Aristotle the Greek philosopher (384–322BC) who analysed tragedy in his *Poetics*. He identified those features that make some tragedies more successful than others, and focuses on the nature of plot and its connections with a moral pattern, the typifying features of the tragic hero, and the play's intensity of focus in time and place. His ideas were reformulated in the seventeenth century and called the **Aristotelian unities;** they were unity of action (the true plot has a cause-and-effect sequence in which there is no irrelevant incident), unity of time (which restricts the duration of the tragedy to one day), and unity of place (which restricts the action to one setting)

characterisation the way in which a writer creates characters in narrative so as to attract or repel our sympathy

chorus a group of characters in ancient Greek tragedies who represent the attitudes of ordinary people in their commentary on the action they witness

classic realist text a text which creates the illusion that it reflects real life and experience by its selection of subject matter and its way of representing that subject matter. The major theme of the classic realist text is subjectivity, and insight into character and psychological processes is central

deconstruction, deconstructive criticism a blanket term for certain radical critical theories which revise and develop structuralism. Many of its ideas originate in the post-structuralist linguistic philosophy developed by Jacques Derrida and it has had a strong influence on literary and critical theory. It is premised on the idea that meaning is not inherent in words nor is it stable; meaning depends on relationships between words within the system of language

dramatic irony occurs when the development of the plot allows the reader to possess more information about what is happening than the characters

feminist feminism is, broadly speaking, a political movement claiming political power and economic equality of women with men. Feminist criticism and scholarship seek to explore and expose the masculine bias in texts and to challenge stereotypical representations of women in literature, as well as to 'recover' the many women writers and texts ignored by the male-biased canon

foreshadow to suggest in advance what will happen later in the novel

formalist all formalist criticism concentrates on form, style and technique to the exclusion of other considerations such as social, political or philosophical aspects; its principle tenet is that the language of literature is different from ordinary language, and that the critic's task is to define this 'literariness'

hierarchy of discourses there are several layers of understanding in a text: the characters will usually only have a limited understanding of events, other characters and even themselves, whereas an omniscient narrator will have an understanding of all events and characters. At the very apex of this pyramid of understanding (or hierarchy of discourses) is the author, the ultimate creator and producer of the text who controls all characters (including the narrator) and the reader's response to them. It is the author who ultimately establishes the truth of the text. The hierarchy of discourses is held to be the distinguishing feature of the classic realist text

imagery in its narrowest sense an 'image' is a word-picture, a description of some visible scene or object. More commonly, however, 'imagery' refers to the figurative language in a piece of literature (metaphors and similes); or all the words which refer to objects and qualities which appeal to the sense and feelings

irony consists of saying one thing and meaning another

Marxist criticism this criticism explores the relationship between the novel and the social, political and economic conditions in which it was produced; the relationship between realism and ideology is central to such analysis

melodrama any kind of writing which relies on sensational happenings, violent action and improbable events

metaphor a metaphor goes further than a comparison between two different things or ideas by fusing them together; one thing is described as being another thing, thus 'carrying over' all its associations

omniscient narrator an omniscient narrator is one who is all seeing and all knowing (god-like, seeing every event and knowing the innermost thoughts and motives of the characters)

pastoral an imaginary world of simple, idealised rural life, in which shepherds and shepherdesses fall in love, enjoying a life of blissful ease, singing songs, playing the flute, etc

patriarchy a social and political system organised so as to give power and prestige to men, and likely to be regarded by men as the natural order of things. A term frequently used in feminist criticism

personification the depiction of things and ideas as if they were human beings, with human attributes and feelings

plot the plan of a literary work, especially of dramas and novels. It suggests a pattern of relationships between events, a web of causation

post-structuralism builds on and refines structuralism. Deconstruction is a significant post-structuralist development

psychoanalytic criticism drawing on Freud's theories of psychoanalysis psychoanalytic criticism analyses literature according to theories of the mind. More recently Jacques Lacan has reworked Freud's psychological theories in terms of structuralism, arguing that the mind is organised around a system of differences, like a language

realism a term used in two main ways: to describe the trend in nineteenth-century literature, especially in prose fiction, which aimed at presenting new truths about people in society in a non-ideal or romantic way; to describe a way of representing real life in literature, which is associated with this historical period

rhetorical question a question asked not for the sake of enquiry, but for emphasis: the writer or speaker expects the reader or audience to be totally convinced about the appropriate reply

Romantic romantic attributes and interests are: (i) a concern to value feeling and emotion rather than the human capacity to reason; (ii) this concern with feeling leads to some of the topics typical of so-called romantic literature: natural, 'primitive' human existence; children who are uncorrupted by society's rigid way of comprehending the world; ghost stories, legends, myths and dreams; (iii) the self. Writers turn in on themselves and try to explain and evaluate their living relationship with the world about them; (iv) a new detailed interest in nature, not for its own sake necessarily, but as a way of coming to understand the self; (v) 'imagination'; Imagination represents the mind's power to create harmonious meaning out of the chaos of impressions, ideas, feelings and memories which inhabit it at any one moment; (vi) a yearning aspiration towards something beyond the ordinary world, not necessarily religious, which gives rise to symbolism, both as a way of looking at the world and as a poetic or literary technique; (vii) a departure from the 'rules of poetry' which dominated the earlier literary period (from 1660 to about 1800, referred to as the 'Neoclassical period'); spontaneity, creativity and the need to allow poems to shape themselves 'organically' (rather than according to rules or reason) are all valued ideals; (viii) rebellion not only against poetic stultification, but against outmoded political institutions

simile a figure of speech in which one thing is said to be like another; similes always contain the words 'like' or 'as'

soliloquy a dramatic convention which allows a character in a play to speak directly to the audience. This convention adds a degree of psychological depth since it provides accurate access to the character's inner-most thoughts, feelings and motives

structuralism structuralists see language not as a neutral means of communication, but as a self-enclosed system and as a code

symbol a symbol is something which represents something else (often an idea or a quality) by analogy or association. Thus white, lion, rose commonly symbolise or represent innocence, courage and beauty

syntax the arrangement of words in their appropriate forms and appropriate order, in order to achieve meaning

theme the abstract subject of a work; its central idea or ideas, which may or may not be explicit or obvious. A text may contain several themes or thematic interests

tragedy a tragedy traces the career and downfall of an individual, and shows in the downfall both the capacities and limitations of human life. The protagonist may be superhuman, a monarch or, in the modern age, an ordinary person

tragic flaw suggests imperfection of character, rather than a mistake of action, as implied by 'error'

Author of this note

Kathryn Simpson is Visiting Lecturer in English at Wolverhampton University and Birmingham University School of Continuing Studies. She received her B.A. and Ph.D. in English from Birmingham University.